The Day God Spoke to Me

JERRY RICHARD CLARK

The Day God Spoke to Me

Trilogy Christian Publishers
A Wholly Owned Subsidiary of Trinity Broadcasting Network
2442 Michelle Drive, Tustin, CA 92780

Copyright © 2024 by Jerry Richard Clark

Scripture quotations marked AMP are taken from the Amplified® Bible (AMP), Copyright © 2015 by The Lockman Foundation. Used by permission. www.Lockman.org.

Scripture quotations marked NASB are taken from the New American Standard Bible® (NASB), Copyright © 1960, 1962, 1963, 1968, 1971, 1972, 1973, 1975, 1977, 1995 by The Lockman Foundation. Used by permission. www.Lockman.org.

Scripture quotations marked Peshitta are taken from the Peshitta Holy Bible from the Ancient Eastern Text, Translated from the Aramaic of the Peshitta. Translated by George M. Lamsa, Copyright 1933 by A. J. Holman Co., Published by A. J, Holman Company. Printed in 1933.

Scripture quotations marked KJV are taken from the King James Version of the Bible. Public domain.

All rights reserved, including the right to reproduce this book or portions thereof in any form whatsoever. For information, address Trilogy Christian Publishing Rights Department, 2442 Michelle Drive, Tustin, CA 92780.

Trilogy Christian Publishing/TBN and colophon are trademarks of Trinity Broadcasting Network.

For information about special discounts for bulk purchases, please contact Trilogy Christian Publishing.

Trilogy Disclaimer: The views and content expressed in this book are those of the author and may not necessarily reflect the views and doctrine of Trilogy Christian Publishing or the Trinity Broadcasting Network.

10 9 8 7 6 5 4 3 2 1
Library of Congress Cataloging-in-Publication Data is available.

ISBN 979-8-89041-869-2
ISBN 979-8-89041-870-8 (ebook)

Dedication

I dedicate this book first and foremost to my God, who entirely changed my life to the better.

My brother Ray, encouraged me to "go for it, make it happen."

My wife Linda, has tolerated the late nights and fixed me meals at odd hours as I worked on this book. Linda's support has been invaluable.

Each of my four children, Wanda, Cheryl, Paul and Janice, have given me valuable encouragement and support in their individual ways.

Acknowledgment

I am grateful to my next door neighbor, Betsy Maring, for the skilled and knowledgeable computer work. Betsy rescued me many times at a moment's notice when my limited computer skills desperately needed help. She was always pleasant, congenial, supportive and encouraging.

Mission Statement

You did not choose me but I chose you, and appointed you, that you should go and bear fruit, and that your fruit should remain, that whatever you ask of the Father in My name, He shall give to you.

— John 15:16 (NASB)

God, I will go anywhere You want me to go, do anything You want me to do, say anything you want me to say to anybody at any time. Just please make your message clear to me, so I don't miss Your communication.

Table of Contents

Dedication iii
Acknowledgment v
Mission Statement vii

Introduction: *Training for God's Call—A Testimonial* . . . 11
Phase 1: *Life Change* 13
Phase 2: *Attending Rhema Bible Training College* 53
Phase 3: *Hospital Ministry* 83
Phase 4: *Evangelism on the Job* 111
Phase 5: *Truck Driving Cross Country* 123
Phase 6: *Ministering in a Church* 155
Phase 7: *Pastoring a Church* 171
Epilogue 199

About the Author 201

Introduction:
Training for God's Call—A Testimonial

On a Sunday night, the pastor of our small Methodist church asked all the teenagers to come down to the altar and pray. All seventeen of us were obedient to comply. As I stood there praying, I sensed a strong stirring within my chest area. I had a strong sense within me that God was speaking to me and calling me to preach. I thought, *Is that really God speaking to me? If so, how can I be certain it is God? Does God even speak to His people in this day and time?*

I don't remember being taught how to recognize the voice of God. We were taught to pray and to talk to God. But I don't remember being taught to hear from God, to listen for His voice. I did not know if it was God speaking to me or not. I remember saying, "God, if that is You speaking to me, I will do anything You want me to do. I will mow the grass, usher in church, or sing in the choir. But I will not be a preacher, and I will not be a missionary to Africa."

All the ten to twelve preachers in our little town of Jenks, Oklahoma, population 1,200, that I was familiar with in 1946–1947 were paid a salary so low that only two or three could afford a car. When I was eight years old, missionaries serving in Africa spoke at the First Christian Church where my family were members. As a young boy, what I understood was that if we didn't send them money each month, they might starve to death in far-off, hot Africa. With the thinking of an eight-year-old boy, I did not want to be broke all my life, and I sure did not want to starve to death in *far-off, hot Africa*. As a strong-willed, outspoken fourteen-year-old boy, I set my conditions for God to use me. I had rejected His calling. As a result, God could not use me. For thirty-one years, I wandered in a spiritual wilderness.

In my early forties, realizing there was something missing in my life, I started an intense, diligent search for whatever that might be. This search lasted about a year to a year and a half. I was not being fulfilled or getting what I wanted in church, so I began to search elsewhere. Part of this search involved attending motivational meetings in major cities. I drove ninety miles to Oklahoma City for a Saturday–Sunday, six-to-eight-hour meeting each day, two hundred miles to Tulsa, Oklahoma, and two hundred fifty miles to Dallas, Texas. During the meetings, nationally known and respected people spoke for close to an hour each. They were all interesting, worthwhile, and inspirational, but I was not receiving what I wanted. I left each of the meetings enthused but still a little bit empty inside, desiring more.

During the period of the "diligent search for what was missing in my life," I had some unusual life-changing spiritual experiences. It became definitely clear that God was again speaking to me and calling me into the ministry. The following is my testimony of seven phases of training for the ministry that God put me through during a fourteen-year period. At forty-five years of age, I had accepted His call! I had found what was missing in my life!

Phase 1
Life Change

God spoke to me in a clear, distinct, and audible voice and told me to "go speak." During the following years, He put me through seven distinct phases of training. This was to prepare me for His call into an evangelistic ministry. During the time these phases were taking place, I did not realize that I was in those separate phases of training. I was well aware that I was daily learning much, much new and potentially useful information. From my viewpoint, I was learning from many different sources. All this learning and spiritual development would be useful when I finished Bible school and entered the ministry. Much later, I became aware that learning for the ministry was from my viewpoint. Training was from God, His viewpoint, direction, and inspiration. God explained the phases of training at the end of the sixth phase. I had anticipated that at the completion of the two-year Bible school teaching at Rhema Bible Training Center, Broken Arrow, Oklahoma, I would move into a full-time traveling ministry. Little did I know what was ahead of me.

Events began to take place over a period of time. Life, as I knew or had experienced it, was changing forever. People who knew me well, those I associated with on a regular basis, often asked, "What has happened to you? Why are you so different?

You don't seem angry anymore. You don't agitate people and create arguments like you used to. What has happened to you?"

The only answer that I knew to give them was that God had spoken to me in an audible voice and told me, "You shall go speak. You shall speak to one or two, four or five, one hundred or two hundred, a thousand or more. You are not restricted to religious organizations. Speak to whoever calls you, whether it be the Boy Scouts, Rotary Club, or whoever it be. You shall speak on truth, responsibility, forgiveness, and the Holy Spirit. In about three years, you will be very busy." This experience occurred on an airplane flight between Atlanta, Georgia, and Oklahoma City, Oklahoma. The time was mid-day, about 1:00 p.m., September 25, 1982. Needless to say, God had caught my attention. His voice was so distinct and audible that I marveled at why everyone on the airplane had not heard Him and was as amazed as me. It became evident to me that the message was for me alone.

During the intensive search for "what was missing in my life" that was mentioned in the introduction, I committed to attending a motivational meeting in Upstate New York. This meeting was spoken of as "The Motivational Meeting of all Motivational Meetings." It was scheduled to be six twelve-to-fourteen-hour days of intense meetings. We were to discover who, what, and why we are as we are. Including travel, the cost totaled $1,500. Obviously, I was in a serious, intense search for what was missing in my life.

The daily, lengthy meetings were exceptional experiences for each of the one hundred and eight participants. Three "leaders" interacted with each of the one hundred and eight participants each day. Freedom of expression was emphasized.

During the week, each participant received a life-changing revelation about themselves.

We had arrived at a rural camp on Sunday afternoon. The following Friday, sessions lasted until 12:00 a.m., midnight. After that was a two-hour-long "social." Saturday morning was to be a brief, leisurely, three-hour wrap-up. Friday night, as people were retiring to their cabins, I felt it worthwhile to walk a trail into the woods and talk to God. I ignorantly felt that I needed to inform God of all the life-changing events that had occurred to me that week.

I came to an opening in the woods of about forty-foot diameter. Here, I began to talk to God and explain all the changes that had taken place within me during this week. I wanted Him to know that I felt He needed to know that I knew how important and life-changing this week had been. In a little while, I noticed a golden glow surrounding me. The golden glow was about hip high, and the density of thick fog. It reached across the opening from tree line to tree line. I was amazed with wonderment as I strolled within the glow. Without realizing I was going to do this, I raised my hands over my head and, with eyes open and face turned up, said, "God, I am Yours. Do what You want with me." This was a physical and vocal expression of full commitment and submission to God. Later, I learned this scripture recorded in Romans 11:29 (NASB): "The gifts and the calling of God are irrevocable." God had not given up on me. God would still use me to minister for Him! After thirty-one years, my ministry call from God was still intact. *Praise God! Praise God!*

I continued to talk to God, not knowing that I should take time to listen in case God wanted to speak to me. Within a few minutes, a vertical circle about four feet in diameter formed about ten feet in front of me. Next, I had a physical sensation that my abdomen slowly opened. When it was wide open, a six-inch wide ray of power formed on the rim of the circle and was directed into my wide-open abdomen. Next to that, a six-inch wide ray of love formed and was directed into me. All around the rim of the circle formed rays of love and power beaming into me. This lasted an estimated two to three minutes. Then the rays stopped, and I had the sensation that my abdomen slowly closed.

I stood there, completely overwhelmed! I had never heard of anything like this. With about five minutes more of me talking to God, I sensed that our conversation was complete. The vertical circle disappeared, and the golden glow began to lift. As it reached about twelve to fifteen feet high, the glow thinned and disappeared. Now I *was all alone!* Later, I became aware that I had experienced the presence of God.

Criticism of My Statements Concerning God's Call

The experience with God that I just described had such a profound impact on my life that I shared the experience with people every day. It seemed that I could not hold it within me.

I soon found out that my testimonial answer regarding the sudden changes in my life was not what people expected or wanted to hear. Many of my friends, acquaintances, and family had been taught against these types of spiritual experiences. It did not fit within their church's doctrinal beliefs. The criticism, scorn, and derisive comments that I received from many of them became almost unbearable.

One day, three members of a doctrinally conservative church, whom I knew well, spent two hours doing their best to convince me how mistaken I was concerning my recent spiritual experiences.

One was an elder in his church congregation. He seemed well-versed in Scripture, especially the teachings of his denomination. I knew very little about Scripture at that time. Concentrating on New Testament Scripture, this elder quoted verse after verse to prove how wrong I was. These three men were very concerned about the sudden changes in my life that I was openly expressing. I am certain that they had my best interests at heart. They did their best to change my thinking. But I knew that I had heard from God in an audible voice. No matter how sincere they were and how strongly they argued, they were not going to change the truth of my recent experience with God. Their conclusion was, "We believe that you believe God spoke to you in an audible voice." There were many other attempts and constant criticism to draw me away from the supernatural experiences that I had had and was continuing to have with God.

Discussing this criticism with a supportive Christian friend, he said, "If those people want a New Testament example about your experience, they should read the experience of Saul on the road to Damascus in Acts Chapters 9 and 22. Jesus spoke to Saul in an audible voice."

Affirmations of the Call

God eliminated any doubt concerning His call on my life. One day, I was visiting with a pastor-friend in his home. During our conversation, God spoke to him with a message for me. The pastor said, "Jerry, you are to start preaching. God just spoke to me and said you are to start preaching. This is the first time that God has given me a message so clear and distinct. God wants you to start preaching!" I replied, "Yes, I understand that. He has spoken directly to me. I am preparing to start preaching."

It was September 25, 1982, when God spoke to me in an audible voice and said, "You shall go speak!" The following January, I woke up bright and alert at 5:00 a.m. In my spirit came this message, "Get up and turn on the TV to channel 47. There is a message for you." Channel 47 is Trinity Broadcasting Network, the local Christian channel. It was cool and chilly in the house but warm and cozy under the blankets. I lay there a few minutes before getting up and dozed back to sleep. Again, instantly, I was awakened, this time close to 5:30 a.m. "Get up and turn on TV channel 47. There is a message for you!" Both times, I was certain it was God speaking into my spirit. This second time, I threw back the covers, hurried into the chilly living room, and quickly turned on TV channel 47. Arthur Blessed, a missionary well known for carrying a cross to many foreign countries and ministering to thousands of people, was standing by a seashore with a mic in his hand. He boldly said, "Go preach the Word!" Then, the program ended.

God had spoken directly to me, then confirmed His message two more times in separate ways. Both ways were unusual to me.

Criticism of me, as I often mentioned the call, was not going to stop me from being obedient to God's call on my life.

The Left Foot of Fellowship

You may be familiar with the common church term "The Right Hand of Fellowship." After giving my testimony in church, I received "The Left Foot of Fellowship"! Members of this church became so unfriendly and socially distant that my family stopped attending there. Fortunately for me, God apparently had a plan and was looking out for my best interests. He immediately took me out of the conservative, restrictive-thinking church that my family and I had been attending. I had given my full testimony of "the golden glow and God speaking to me in an audible voice" from the pulpit to the entire congregation. This testimony was against their church doctrine. I was no longer welcome in that church. Through a set of circumstances that I believe was orchestrated by God, He put me in a church that freely expressed love, joy, peace, and the power of the Holy Spirit in daily living.

That church was a Pentecostal, Charismatic, full gospel church.

You may ask, exactly what is a Pentecostal, Charismatic, full gospel church? My definition is this: Pentecostal refers to the Day of Pentecost as described in Acts 2:1–4. Pentecost is a Greek word referring to fifty days after the Jewish celebration of the Feast of the Passover held annually in Jerusalem, Israel. In that portion of the New Testament, one hundred twenty followers of the Jewish Rabbi, Jesus, both men and women, were meeting regularly for prayer and discussion in a second-floor room in Jerusalem.

> *One day there came a sound like a mighty rushing wind. It filled the whole house where they were sitting. There appeared tongues as of fire resting on each one of them. They were all filled [baptized] with the Holy Spirit and began to speak with other tongues [other languages] as the Spirit gave them utterance.*
>
> — Acts 2:1–3 (NASB)

Acts 2:1–13 makes references to what praying in tongues is. Verse 6 states, "The people who had gathered in the street were bewildered because they were each one hearing them speak in their own language." Verse 7 says, "They were amazed and marveled saying, 'Why, are not all of these Galileans who are speaking?'" Verse 8 states, "And how is it that we each hear them in our own language to which we were born?" Praying in tongues, then, is praying to God in a language spoken by people in a foreign country yet unlearned by the person praying. This is done "as the Spirit gives them utterance" (Acts 2:4, NASB).

The people gathered in the street were from fifteen different countries. They had gathered in Jerusalem for a popular annual Jewish feast. People from each country spoke their own language or a dialect of a local language. People from Galilee spoke their own Galilean language or dialect.

A crowd had gathered in the street because of this "noise like a mighty rushing wind." Peter, one of the original twelve disciples chosen by Jesus, stepped out on the veranda and preached to the large crowd. They had gathered, wondering, "What has caused this noise like a mighty rushing wind?" Peter spoke with boldness and confidence uncommon to Jewish rabbis, scribes, and other leaders. This was the result of the Holy Spirit filling and inspiring Peter for the purpose of the occasion. About 3,000 people believed this message of Jesus as the Jewish Messiah and received their salvation that day.

Full gospel merely refers to the gifts of the Holy Spirit being in full operation with His power and authority in this day and time. These gifts are described in 1 Corinthians 12:1–11. Full gospel also includes both the Old and New Testament's teaching of God's power and love in our daily lives. It means God's supernatural power is available to operate in today's Spirit-filled Christians' daily lives as it did in the first-century church and among the original twelve apostles chosen by Jesus.

Charismatic comes from the Greek term "charisma," which refers to the gifts of the Holy Spirit in action. My definitions of the terms "full gospel" and "Charismatic" are nearly synonymous.

This type of preaching, with uncommon boldness and confidence, was being presented consistently at the church where we had become members by Pastor Billy Walker. All members of this church were baptized in the Holy Spirit with the evidence in common of speaking in tongues. The gifts of the Holy Spirit were in operation in every service. Was this ever different from what we had previously experienced in the various churches that we had attended throughout our lifetimes?

For several years, my wife and I had been associated with a very conservative church denomination that taught that the gifts of the Holy Spirit (including praying in tongues) had ended with the death of the apostles. Any expression of this today, therefore, had to be false.

Their doctrine stated that "praying in tongues" was of the devil.

After receiving the baptism of the Holy Spirit with a fluent "prayer language," I wrote one of these pastors a letter. When we were members of the church he pastored, this pastor had become a close friend. Once, he adamantly told me, "Stay away from those people who speak in tongues. That is of the devil." I explained in my letter that after searching both the Old and New Testaments carefully, I was unable to find any scripture that stated, "tongues were of the devil." Neither could I find a scripture that stated tongues spoken in any generation had ended. I explained to the pastor that during my younger years, living somewhat unrestrained, I had been in bars where some of the people were over-indulging with hardly any noticeable restraint. Some of them would become drunk and foul-mouthed. Men were tempting women, and women were tempting men to a night in bed together. Obviously, sin was rampant. But I never saw anyone praying in tongues. I had worked on construction jobs where hard-working men were very foul-mouthed and used very sinful language. But I never heard any of them praying in tongues. Surely, if praying in tongues were of the devil, people over-indulging in the bars and the foul-mouthed men on the construction jobs would pray in tongues also. The pastor never replied to my letter.

Gotebo, Oklahoma: Spiritual Power in Church

The Pentecostal-style church that I previously mentioned was in Gotebo, Oklahoma.

Gotebo is a small town of about 300 people located in the middle of wheat farms in Southwestern Oklahoma. The town was named after a Kiowa Native American chief. It was a twenty-five-mile one-way drive from our home to the church at Gotebo. At New Life Christian Fellowship in the town of Gotebo, we found the love, joy, and peace that I had heard preached about but never experienced in previous church congregations that we had attended.

During a Wednesday night service, Pastor Billy Walker commented, "Many of us are out of the Baptist Church. On Wednesday nights, the Baptist Church has lots of testimonies. We still think that is a good idea. Who has a testimony to share with us?" Hands went up all over the congregation. People gave testimonies typical of this. "I was having this problem and did not know what to do. So, I got by myself and talked to God. God told me what to do. I did what He said, and the problem was eliminated." I sat there listening and thinking, *These people hear from God. They have each spoken with sincerity about talking to God and hearing from Him. This is new to me. I will give my full testimony once more. If I get the criticism that I have received everywhere else, then I am going to keep quiet and not give it anymore.* Up went my hand. The pastor called on me. I went up front and gave my full testimony. As I spoke, these people relived the experience with me. I had found a church home! We began to drive the fifty-mile round trip to Gotebo twice on Sunday and again on Wednesday night, hardly ever missing.

We were learning so very, very much. As we learned, we began to realize how much we needed to know. There were numerable biblical-ministry subjects that we were vaguely familiar with but not knowledgeable enough to use and certainly not teach. Pastor Billy taught about the Holy Spirit and the gifts of the Holy Spirit. We had heard sermons about these subjects but knew practically nothing about them. We became enthused and excited as we listened to his teaching about the supernatural power of God operating in our lives. Jesus said, "Truly, truly, I say to you, he who believes in Me, the works that I do shall he do also; and greater works than these shall he do; because I go to the Father" (John 14:12, NASB). Billy taught that "Jesus was speaking to His disciples. A disciple is a student of a teacher. We are this generation's disciples. Through the power of the Holy Spirit, we [you, Jerry, and Linda Clark] can do the things that Jesus did." *What! This is a reality for me?* This was overwhelming and mind-boggling to me. He continued, "Jesus, as a man, operated with the power of the Holy Spirit and did miracles. The Holy Spirit is still here. We as Spirit-filled Christians are to operate with the same power of the Holy Spirit and do miracles."

Consistently, Billy would have a "word from the Lord" and deliver that message to church members. Strangers regularly attended services. Often, at some time during his message or at the end of it, Pastor Billy would speak into their lives very accurately with information that the Holy Spirit had given him. Many times, the person would reply how greatly blessed they were as a result of the message delivered.

When I realized this supernatural power was for real, I wanted it! To learn about this power, how to recognize and when to use it, I questioned the pastor. Billy told me what scriptures to study in various parts of the Bible, what books to read, and who were reputable authors, and he encouraged me.

Periodically, he would have a "message" for Linda and me. To me, this was *big stuff!* I still had questions and doubts about ministering in this manner. Yet, I wanted to and sensed that God wanted me to. Where was I going to find the courage, boldness, and faith to minister in this manner? My life was changing. I thought it needed to change a lot more before I could minister as I understood God wanted me to. I knew that God wanted me to preach, and I wanted to preach. However, I did not know how to prepare a sermon and sensed that I lacked enough faith.

Two nights before God spoke to me in the audible voice, I had spent about two hours in communion, including prayer, with Him. During that period of intimacy with Him, He baptized me in the Holy Spirit. I was different! I could not describe how I was different. I just knew that I was different! I felt completely empty of my previous self. I was comfortable and at peace with the emptiness but puzzled by it. After a few lessons about the baptism of the Holy Spirit at the Gotebo church, I realized, "Oh, this is what happened to me. No wonder I am so different, so empty of self."

Experiencing the Prayer Language

I soon became aware that I needed the prayer language that I was hearing taught about and commonly used in this church. It would be of spiritual benefit to me. Jude 20–21 states that praying in tongues will build up your faith and keep you in the love of God. First Corinthians 14:4 (NASB) states, "One who speaks in a tongue edifies [enlightens] himself." I had to overcome the previous teaching about this prayer language being "evil, of the devil." Once that was accomplished, out of me flowed a spirit prayer language.

My wife, Linda, soon received the baptism also. She started praying fluently in a prayer language. Her experience was independent of mine. She thought that the only way for her to receive the baptism of the Holy Spirit and prayer language was if our pastor, Billy Walker, prayed for her. One Sunday night, a guest speaker prayed for several guests, and they each received their prayer language. Linda waited until Pastor Billy could pray for her a few nights later. He laid hands on her and prayed, but no language came forth. A few weeks later, Linda and I had driven the two hundred and fifty miles to Dallas, Texas, to attend a motivational meeting. Late at night, she was driving and praying about "that prayer language." I was sound asleep. Suddenly, out came her prayer language. She was excited about this and "prayed in the spirit" until I woke up. Being shy about this, she stopped. She quickly found out that she could start and stop the language anytime she wanted.

Linda had another experience that excited her. Driving home from school with our six-year-old daughter, Janice, in the car, she began singing in her spirit language. After a few minutes, this thought startled her, *Maybe I am not supposed to sing in the spirit?* She stopped singing.

Later, Pastor Billy assured her that according to 1 Corinthians 14:15, singing in the spirit is praising and worshiping God. It is proper to do so.

Linda—The Spirit-Filled Cowgirl

During the winter, there had been a bad snow-ice storm in Southwest Oklahoma, where we lived. Snow was about six inches deep, with a crust of ice one to two inches on top of the snow. Snow drifts measured two feet deep in much of the area. We were living on Linda's dad's farm. He had about twenty cows that had to be cared for with water and fed daily.

Late one afternoon, when I came in from work, Linda's car was in the driveway, but I could not find Linda. The cows were not in the corral for the night. I climbed as high as safely possible on the wood rail fence to see over the crest of a low hill in the pasture. I could hear Linda's voice being carried across the crusted ice. As I watched, the cows wandered over the crest of the hill. They were headed for the corral, where there was food and water for them. Behind the cows walked Linda in her snow boots and insulated coveralls. She was pleasantly singing in her spirit prayer language as she herded the cows. At a cross fence, there was a gate. All the cows turned left through the gate headed for the corral except one contrary cow. She turned right, apparently headed toward another corner of the pasture. Linda stopped singing, pointed to the cow, and began to speak in her prayer language with a strong, commanding tone in her voice. The errant cow stopped, turned around, and walked along the fence line, through the gate, and into the corral. I watched all this action from my high perch on the fence.

When Linda closed the gate, puzzled by her unusual action, I asked, "What were you doing singing in the spirit as you walked behind the cows?" Linda innocently replied, "My angels and I were herding the cows! When one cow left the herd, I stopped singing and told one of my angels to stop that cow and herd it back to the corral. My angels are good cowboys. I always have them help me when I need them." Obviously,

God honors innocent faith. I climbed down the fence, both amused and amazed.

Another Angel Cowboy Story

One Sunday morning, our family was in the car, traveling down the long driveway and going to church at Gotebo. We suddenly saw a frustrating and emotionally upsetting situation! The cows were out of the pasture and in the fresh green wheat! For a wheat farmer, this is a strong *no-no*. I stopped the car and quickly ran to the barn where the tractor was stored. As I left the car, I could hear Linda praying in her spirit language.

I quickly threw two bales of old dry hay on the tractor hay forks and drove down the driveway near where the cows were. Linda was still intently praying in tongues. As I turned the tractor around, the cows stopped eating the foot-high, green, juicy, tasty wheat, then followed the tractor with its two bales of last year's dry hay on the forks. This action by cows is unheard of. They naturally prefer that juicy, green wheat over the old dry hay.

After the cows were back in the pasture, the tractor parked in the barn, and I was in the car again, I commented to Linda, "That was sure unusual. I have never heard of cows easily leaving green, fresh wheat and following old, dry hay as if they preferred to eat it."

Linda replied, "When I was talking in tongues, I was consciously telling my angels to round up the cows and make them follow the dry hay to the corral." We both chuckled at that experience. It clearly revealed to me that Linda was progressing in the knowledge of God's Word and authority. Her faith was developing as surely as mine. Yes, "the *two* of us were *one*."

Searching for Bible Truths

We had learned that the Bible is God's written truth. Recognizing this, we began searching the Bible for God's truth in many, many different subjects. Individual church teachings that differ from other church teachings on the same subject are often influenced by the church leadership who is doing the teaching. It is easy for any individual teacher to make a mistake as he studies, no matter how sincere he may be. The Bible never changes. We became dependent on Bible truths.

We also became stalwart members of the "Gotebo church." It became known as the "spiritual hotspot" of Southwest Oklahoma. People regularly drove up to fifty miles one-way from all directions to get spiritually fed at this spiritual oasis. The two years spent under the teaching of Pastor Billy Walker at Gotebo gave Linda and me a foundational Bible teaching of God's "truths" of supernatural power in a Christian's daily life.

Pastor Billy Walker operated with the gifts of the Holy Spirit consistently. When I was satisfied in my own mind that the gifts were for real in this day and time, I wanted them! I wanted a thorough knowledge of the gifts and what made them operate. I wanted supernatural miracles operating in my life and ministry. With this desire began a long, intensive study of God, Jesus, the Holy Spirit, and His gifts that continues to this very day. No one ever reaches the level where they know all there is to know about those subjects. Even today, after forty years of ministry and at eighty-five years of age, it still is inspirational and exciting when the Holy Spirit uses me to operate His gifts through in some manner.

I learned that the Holy Spirit's gifts are His gifts. He chooses when, where, and through whom He will use His gifts.

If the gifts were mine (man's gifts), I would go to the hospitals, use the gifts of healing, get everyone healed, and send them home. But the gifts are not mine to use when I choose.

My serious question was, "Is it really possible for me, Jerry Clark, the small-town Okie, to do the things that Jesus did? Could I heal the sick, cast out demons, raise people from the dead, and do even greater things than these?" I could if I would follow the example of Jesus and operate as He did. Jesus would often spend all night or longer communing with His Father, God. God would tell Jesus what, when, and how events or situations were going to take place. He also told Jesus what to do in those circumstances. The key to the operation of God's supernatural power operating in my life, then, is consistent, intimate communing with God. It is He who has the spiritual power, not any man or woman. God will use individuals as He chooses. A close study of the New Testament will support what I have just stated. As an example, Romans 4:17 (NASB) states, "Even God who gives life to the dead and calls into being that which does not exist." Recorded in John 14:12 (NASB), Jesus states, "Truly, truly, I say to you, he who believes in me, the works that I do shall he do also; and greater works than these shall he do; because I go to the Father." I began to realize that if I accept what God has stated in the Bible as truth and reality for me and operate in faith, then yes, through the authority of Jesus and the power of the Holy Spirit, I can do the things that Jesus did and greater works than these. But what are greater works than healing the sick, casting out demons, and raising someone from the dead? This question reveals another study to find that answer.

I learned that Jesus was baptized in water and then baptized in the Holy Spirit (Matthew 3:11–17).

After those events in His life, Jesus began to do the supernatural, the miraculous. It is not recorded in the Bible that Jesus did anything supernatural before He was baptized in water, then the "Holy Spirit came upon Him like a dove" (Luke 3:22, NASB). This event describes a total covering and anointing of Jesus by the Holy Spirit. From there on, Jesus operated with the power of the Holy Spirit. If I wanted the supernatural power of God operating in my life, then I must follow the example of Jesus receiving God's supernatural power.

Definitions

In this testimonial, I often refer to God, Jesus, the Holy Spirit, and the Bible. Who or what are they?

Except for the Bible, which is a book, we cannot physically see them with our eyes as we see other humans. So, how can we be sure they exist? How can we be confident they are active with authority and power to accomplish things as I describe in this "book"? I offer the following descriptions and answers.

WHAT IS THE BIBLE?

A book written by more than forty men over a period of 1,500 years. With each man writing as God inspired him, there are a total of sixty-six individual "books." All sixty-six books are compiled in what Christians call "the Bible." This book is divided into two primary sections: the Old and the New Testaments. The word "Testament" can also be defined as "covenant." The "Old is separated from the New" by the story of the life and teachings of Jesus, the Son of God.

Genesis, the first book of the Old Testament, was written approximately 3,500 years ago. The last book written is Revelation, written by John, the Apostle of Jesus, about AD 90 or approximately 1,930 years ago. "They each wrote with an unusual harmony despite the difference of times in which they lived. How could this be possible? Through the mystery and miracle of divine inspiration!" (*Foundations of Pentecostal Theology*, Guy P. Duffield and Nathaniel Van Cleave, pages 19–21).

I have read that most religions are man's efforts to find God and deal with, work with, and serve the God that they find. Judaism and Christianity are the story of God creating man and dealing with him.

WHO IS GOD?

The Creator of "the heavens," earth, and everything in and on the earth (Genesis 1). God's greatest creation was mankind. Genesis 1:26 (NASB) states, "Let us make man in Our own image, according to Our likeness." Verse 27 states, "And God created man in His own image, in the image of God He created him; male and female He created them." Verse 31 states, "And God saw all that He had made, and behold, it was very good." The book of Proverbs, written hundreds of years later by a different writer, supports these statements of creation as recorded in Proverbs 3:19–20.

God is a three-part being: Father, Son, and Holy Spirit. God created man in His own image, a three-part being—spirit, soul, and body.

God is a "Spirit" (John 4:24). A spirit is inanimate, with no physical body to inhabit, but has a soul (mind, will, emotions, and memory) to think with. A human spirit controls or influences the body it inhabits. The spirit gives the body life (John 6:63). The human body with a human spirit, then, is alive. If the spirit leaves the body, the body is immediately dead (James 2:26).

WHO IS JESUS?

"Son of God." God sent Jesus to earth in a supernatural manner. His mother, Mary, was engaged to a man named Joseph. As recorded in Luke 1:6–28, an angel (messenger from God—Hebrews 1:13) appeared to Mary and told her that she would "bear a son and you shall name Him Jesus" (Luke 1:13, NASB). Mary asked the angel, "How can this be since I am a virgin?" The Bible speaks metaphorically here and quotes the angel as saying, "The Holy Spirit will come upon you, and the power of the Most High will overshadow you; and for that reason, the holy offspring shall be called the Son of God. For nothing will be impossible with God" (Luke 1:35–37, NASB).

WHO IS THE HOLY SPIRIT?

He is a "who" and not an "it." The Holy Spirit is spoken of as the third person of the Trinity, the Trinity being described as the Father, Son, and Holy Spirit. Each has its individual functions. Among many definitions and descriptions, both biblical and by man, I will briefly use these. God is the Creator. Jesus is the Redeemer, Savior of man, and Teacher of a godly lifestyle. The Holy Spirit is the action of God with power. In biblical study, we find that the Holy Spirit does not have a body as Jesus did. But He does possess a personality and emotions. He is referred to as the "Person of the Holy Spirit."

Action and power: Genesis 1:2 (NASB) states, "The Spirit of God was moving over the waters." God put the Holy Spirit in action before He spoke and took other action to recreate the surface of the earth.

Acts 1:8 (NASB) states, "You shall receive power when the Holy Spirit comes upon you." Matthew 28:19 (NASB) states, "Go therefore and make disciples of all the nations, baptizing them in the name of the Father, Son, and Holy Spirit."

Faith: With all the problems of mankind in this world, how can we accept that the Bible, including all its stories of people in various countries and God's miracles or supernatural events during the past 3,500 years, is true? I will relate a few of my own experiences. Many times, during the past forty years of ministry serving God, I have had conversations with God. How did I know it was God? Whatever God speaks to me will be supported in the Bible. He would tell me of upcoming events, and those events would happen exactly as He said at the time that He told me. I have asked Him questions and He would answer me. It is reminiscent of conversations with my daughters and son on the telephone. Because of our relationship and fellowship, I recognize their voices. I can trust what they tell me. We live in truth and love each other.

Because of my relationship with God, I know that I can trust what He tells me. Because of consistent fellowship with Him, I recognize His voice and the truth of His statements to me.

For me, that is faith!

Now, let's go back to my story of being called into the ministry and events that contributed to life-changing lessons.

Pastor Billy Walker invited me to attend a Full Gospel Businessmen's meeting in Clinton, Oklahoma, four weeks after God had spoken to me. Clinton was a 100-mile round trip from where I lived. I was hesitant about driving that far to attend a meeting, but Pastor Billy was strongly encouraging. He said, "There is always good praise and worship music, and someone always gives an interesting testimony about his spiritual life." At Billy's insistence, I drove to Clinton to attend the meeting, taking my ten-year-old son, Paul, for company. The congregational singing was strong and uplifting as promised by Pastor Billy. The featured speaker was a retired Army officer from Ohio. He was giving an interesting presentation of his spiritual life when, in the middle of a sentence, he stopped and looked over the audience. Then he spoke with a loud, bold, commanding voice, "God just told me to give these two scriptures. I don't know who they are for or why they need them, but I do know that God just now told me to give them! Matthew 10:19–20 and Ephesians 3:16–17." Then, he continued with his testimony as though nothing unusual had happened.

I thought to myself, *That is the most arrogant statement I have ever heard a preacher make.*

Imagine him interrupting his own presentation and speaking out so boldly and saying, "God just spoke to me." I have never in my lifetime seen nor heard a preacher do that before. But it was interesting anyway. I wrote the scriptures on a printed meeting program for future reference.

After the meeting, I reviewed the scriptures in my Bible. Both scriptures answered questions that I had prayed for two weeks. I had questioned God, "You told me to go preach, and I want to go preach. But God, I don't know how to prepare a sermon. I can't quote scriptures. What will I tell an audience when I get an invitation to preach? How do I even select a subject?" It is not that I had stepped out into the unknown; God had thrust me into the unknown! I felt totally lost, not knowing which direction to take to make some sense out of this "spiritual and mental wilderness." I didn't even have a "machete" to chop a path through this wilderness. *Do I go forward, whichever direction that is? Do I go backward, right, left, up, or down?* I was confused yet happily lost in this spiritual wilderness.

During a long-distance telephone conversation with my brother Ray, I told him that the responsibility of ministering was too great. "I just do not have the faith to minister to people. What I say or do not say, what I do or do not do, may determine whether a person goes to heaven or hell when their physical body dies. The risk of sending somebody to hell is too great. It was okay with me to influence boys and girls when I was a high school teacher and football coach. That influence was for their time here on earth. But God wants me to influence people for eternity. I don't have faith for that. God should have chosen somebody else."

Ray replied, "Let's take a look at that! You told me that God spoke to you in an audible voice and told you to go preach. You told me that God still speaks to you in a still, quiet voice, through various Bible scriptures and through other people."

I replied, "Yes, that is true."

"Jerry, I was in the Army for fourteen years. Through that time, I was stationed on several Army bases in the USA and foreign countries. I always attended church services wherever I was stationed. I have never in my life heard a preacher say,

'God spoke to me in an audible voice and told me to go preach.' You just told me that God should have chosen somebody else. You are saying that God made a mistake. Who are you to contradict God?"

Clang! Clang! It was as if somebody had hit me full force right in the face with a cold, wet towel. *Oh!* God must have a reason for speaking to me in an audible voice and commanding me to "go speak…" *I better start studying, learning, and stepping out with whatever level of faith I have and do what God tells me to do.*

I wondered, *Will my previous formal education help my preaching preparation, skills, and effectiveness?* In my college education, I have both bachelor's and master's degrees, plus thirty-four semester hours toward a doctorate in Public Education. Two additional courses would have qualified me to be a public school superintendent. An additional thirty semester hours would be approximately enough to qualify for a doctorate degree in Public Education. In what manner would this previous formal education assist me as a minister? Would it make any difference at all?

One Sunday night, a guest evangelist spoke at the Gotebo church. He presented a very interesting message and was very effective in ministering to people. He would pray for someone, lay hands on them, and they would fall to the floor under the power of the Holy Spirit. I was impressed with his ministry authority and the spiritual power obviously flowing through this minister. The man was only about five foot seven inches tall, with a lean and rugged physical body. Obviously, he had little formal education.

As he presented his testimony, it went something like this: "I quit school in the seventh grade and went to work on construction jobs. I have never had any more education nor learned how to speak in front of an audience. God called me to preach, and I don't know how. I never learned to read well, but I study my Bible and do what I understand God wants me to do." Of course, there was more testimony that I don't recall now. I was impressed with the man's sincerity, integrity, and humility. His love of God, desire to do the works of Jesus, and submission to the Holy Spirit were obvious. God's Holy Spirit worked through him strongly and effectively. I was impressed!

My conclusion: There may be some parts of my formal education that will help in the ministry, but I had better follow this man's characteristics of expressing God's love to people. I need to study humility, sincerity, and integrity. I had better study the life and ministry of Jesus and apply His characteristics to my life and ministry. I had much to learn!

I am a man who was raised to think and act independently. Since high school, I had primarily made my own decisions and did what I wanted to do or thought was best for myself. Now, I was forty-five years old and had a wife, four children, and a business to operate. An entirely new ministry life was ahead of me. Concerning this new life, I did not even know how to start or which way to go. All I could do was cry out to God for help! Like the artist-painter, I needed to start somewhere, somehow! If I don't start, then I have nothing to finish, and nothing will be accomplished. If I start and what I have started is wrong, bad, or ineffective, then I can always change to something that I perceive to be effective. But I must start!

Reviewing scriptures, the Full Gospel Businessmen's speaker gave Matthew 10:19–20, which had some answers for me. "Do not become anxious about how or what you shall speak; for it shall be given you in that hour what you are to speak. For it is not you who speak, but it is the Spirit of your Father who speaks in you" (Matthew 10:19, NASB).

Within the first few weeks after God called me to "go speak..." I came to realize that within His calling and service, I knew nothing. He knew everything. He had called me to preach, but I did not know how to preach nor be influential or effective with a church audience. I made this commitment to God, "I will preach anywhere, anytime, to anybody, but You are going to have to speak through me. I am not going to make speeches on religious subjects!" I believe this is what God wanted to hear from me: total commitment and total reliance on Him.

I had also told God, "I now see preachers operating with the gifts of the Holy Spirit and supernatural things happen. I don't have that kind of power or faith to do what they do or say. I am not going to copy what they do or say. God, I don't have the faith or power to preach. How am I going to learn all I need to know? When I get an invitation to preach, what will I tell the audience?"

I reviewed Ephesians 3:16–17 (NASB), which states, "that He would grant you according to the riches of His glory to be strengthened with power through His Spirit in the inner man, so that Christ may dwell in you heart through faith." So that is how it will happen. God's Holy Spirit will speak in me; then, I will speak out the message. God will strengthen me with power using His Spirit so that Christ may dwell in my heart through faith. I must have the courage to step out and speak out. The Holy Spirit in me will guide me as to what to do and speak. That sounds simple enough. Where is my courage? How do I develop enough courage and faith to accomplish what I understand God wants me to do? How will I know when enough is enough, however much enough might be?

After forty years of ministry, I am still a little nervous or apprehensive immediately before I preach. Once I start talking, the Holy Spirit takes over, and I say what I have prepared or what seems natural. The Holy Spirit speaks through me according to God's Word. He inspires me with what to say.

God speaks to people in different ways. I have experienced His audible voice, Him speaking to me through His written Word, the Bible, and prophetically through other people. Also, He has spoken directly into me, the spirit man, with that still, quiet voice. These were exciting experiences for this new preacher.

Bible Versions

Linda and I were daily spending much time reading our Bibles. Even though we both had attended church all our lives, we were not knowledgeable of the Bible at all. After the baptism of the Holy Spirit, God opened our spirits with a strong desire to learn what He wanted us and His other people to know. He also opened our minds (souls) to understand His Word, the Bible. This was critically important to both of us. If I am going to preach, I must understand the Bible as I read it so I can accurately relay its truths to an audience.

In England during the 1500s and 1600s, it was common to use words like "thee," "thou," and add "ith" to some words.

In today's American English language, those words are not commonly used. When reading the King James version of the Bible, those terms seemed foreign and somehow confused me. For me, the NASB was much easier to understand.

Reading the King James Bible, I continually had to stop and interpret what it was saying. This made reading or studying the Bible hard work and time-consuming. I discussed this with several pastors and other Christians whom I respected for their experience and knowledge. I reviewed several modern language versions they had recommended. Eventually, I settled on the New American Standard Bible. It is written in today's modern American language. It is also considered to be one of the most accurate modern language Bibles. I could easily understand it. This Bible fits my criteria. After forty years of ministry, the New American Standard Bible is still my primary reading and study Bible.

In addition, for comparison reference, I use the Amplified Bible, King James Version, and Eastern Orthodox Christian Bible. The Eastern Bible was originally written in Aramaic. It was translated by George Lamsa into American English in 1933. It is a complete translation of the Peshitta, the authorized Bible of the Christian Church of the East. There is very little difference between the Peshitta and NASB. One differing example is the Lord's Prayer. As recorded in Matthew 6:13 in both the NASB and KJV, "And lead us not into temptation…" The Peshitta records, "And do not let us enter into temptation…" Also, I have other Bible versions in my library. When writing or preparing a sermon I commonly use two or more of these versions to assure clarity and accuracy.

The knowledge gained when studying the differences in the various Bible versions has proven to be valuable and useful information through the years.

New Preaching Experiences

Those first few months, I was anxious to preach. In my youthful ignorance, I expected an invitation any day soon. Looking back, it was good that I did not get an invitation. The experience would have been a "train wreck." Finally, after more than a year, I received an invitation to deliver my testimony at a Full Gospel Businessmen's meeting. The meeting went well, but my lack of preaching skills was apparent to me. There is a unique excitement and enthusiasm that comes with the Holy Spirit's anointing. It is easy to lose all sense of timing and speak too long. Timing, when preaching, was another lesson that I obviously needed to learn.

A few weeks later, I received a second Full Gospel Businessmen invitation. That week, the demands of my steel building construction business required me to work twelve to fourteen hours each day.

Finally, one Saturday at noon, I was home with a little time to rest before the 7:00 p.m. meeting. A friend called. His wife was sick. She wanted me to come to their house and pray for her.

Previously, she had asked me to pray for her when sick and would receive her healing. I suspected her faith was more in me rather than in God. Because of her "desperation," I hurriedly drove to their house. This entire ministry and travel time would take about one hour. Still, I would have a few hours to rest and prepare for the evening presentation.

I was tired, aggravated, and frustrated because of the time interruption. Driving to their house, I began to pray. "God, I am scheduled to speak at 7:00 p.m. I feel obligated to minister to this lady, and it will take up an hour of my time. Then, it is another one-hour drive to where I speak. I have been working twelve to fourteen hours each day this week. This has not allowed me time to pray or read my Bible in preparation for the meeting tonight. I know that I am to give my testimony. But God, what kind of message do You want me to weave into my testimony? Please give me some scriptures and tell me how to use them."

I was anticipating some profound, audience-attention-catching, life-changing scriptures that I was only vaguely familiar with. Immediately, two familiar scriptures came to me. Disappointed, I rudely blurted out, "Great, God. Everybody knows those scriptures. How am I going to blend them into my testimony?"

Don't ever speak rudely to God!

One of the scriptures God gave me was Philippians 4:13 (KJV), "I can do all things through Christ who strengthens me." I suppose this happened in the spirit realm, but it could not ever be more physically real. God grabbed me by the shoulders and shook me like a little child. He very strongly said, "Jerry, you can do nothing without Christ and His strength!"

I learned that lesson very quickly and very well! I have never spoken rudely to God since that experience.

I prayed for my friend. She immediately received her healing from God. The meeting that night went well. God is— was faithful even with my youthful, foolish lack of courtesy and spiritual experience. My knowledge of His character greatly increased also.

Obedience and Timing

So many lessons to be learned. At the time, God spoke to me with the message to "go speak…" I was in the steel-building construction business. A local farmer had contracted with me to build a foundation that he planned to move and set up an existing building on. Another local young man, Randy Powers, owned a ditching machine, backhoe-loader, and dump truck. I had a verbal agreement with Randy to dig the foundation footings and haul fill dirt for all the steel buildings that I built. That morning, Randy was digging the ditches so I could pour concrete into them for the building footings. Randy was a Spirit-filled Christian. The only other man on the job was Ralph Ratliff, also a Spirit-filled Christian and member of the Gotebo church. The three of us created a fairly strong Christian atmosphere.

The morning that we started work, Randy told me that he wanted to get it done as early as possible. "I have a sore throat and can barely talk." His sister, a nurse, had checked his throat and concluded that Randy had strep throat. To fulfill my needs, Randy agreed to dig the footings before he went to the doctor for treatment. I was curious as to how badly the throat was infected. At my request, Randy opened his mouth and stuck out his tongue so I could see inside his throat. His throat was bright red and covered with small, white pus pockets. It was easy to see that he definitely had strep throat.

Randy started digging. I asked God if He wanted me to lay hands on Randy and pray for him so God could heal him. God spoke to me in my spirit and said, "Yes. Do it right now." In my spiritually youthful ignorance, I replied, "God, as soon as he finishes this trench in twenty to thirty minutes, I will do that." God spoke to me again, "I said pray for Randy right now!" I understood and, this time, was quickly obedient. I hurried to my service truck, opened my Bible, and quickly reviewed three healing scriptures that God had given me.

I walked near the digging machine, got Randy's attention, and gave him a physical sign to kill the engine. The muffler had broken off during the previous job, and Randy had not installed a new muffler. The engine noise was so loud that he could not hear me talk. We had agreed to use sign language because of the loud engine noise. I asked Randy, "May I pray for your throat so God can heal it?" Randy worked up some saliva in his dry, sore throat and managed to say, "Yes." I laid my hands on Randy's throat, quoted the healing scriptures, prayed for him, and started to leave. Randy struggled to say, "Thank you." He then continued to dig with the loud engine blasting our ears.

In a few minutes, I needed to tell Randy something concerning the digging. To get his attention, I threw and hit him with a small dirt clod. He looked up, and I loudly yelled, "Kill the engine." Randy yelled back very loudly and said, "I can't understand you. The engine is too loud!" More sign language. He killed the engine. We discussed the digging issue, both of us talking in normal tones and volume. Then I asked, "Randy, have you noticed that you are talking normally?" Surprised and amazed, he said, "Well, I sure am. God must have healed me!" We were both amazed and excited about God's quick action.

A few minutes later, the farmer and a friend of his drove up to the job. They were both pleasant and friendly, but the air "turned blue" with their foul language. The entire spiritual atmosphere changed with their presence. My thoughts were, *Oh, God knew they were on the way to the job. He wanted me to minister to Randy while the spiritual atmosphere was "clean."* My lesson was, "Be obedient to God's timing. Don't delay or attempt to do what God tells me on my schedule or convenience." Later that afternoon, I saw Randy in town. I asked, "Randy, did you go to the doctor to get your throat treated?" He replied, "No, I didn't need to. God healed me this morning on the job."

An invitation to preach at a church came to me. The church was in the town of Cyril, Oklahoma, about one-hour drive from home. Linda and I were about twenty minutes early. No one was at the church. At the exact time for church services to begin, the pastor arrived. Within the next twenty minutes, about eighty Native Americans and twenty White people filled the church building. The service went very well. Preaching completed, I gave an altar call for prayer needs. Six people came forward. I laid hands on each of them in turn and prayed in support of their stated needs. An older man in the prayer line told me, "I have arthritis in my arm and shoulder joints. The pain is so bad that I cannot use a hammer or screwdriver and do maintenance on my house." I thought, *This man is expecting a miracle! How do I pray for him?* I laid my hands on the man and started praying in tongues. Without realizing it or making a conscious decision to do so, I switched to English and said, "You foul demon, come out of this man, in Jesus's name." He started walking back to his seat. As I began to pray for the next person, I noticed that the audience's attention was on the man I had just prayed for rather than on the ministry praying taking place. The man was twisting his arms and hands with tears streaming down his face. *No pain!* A demon spirit had been causing the arthritis-type pain. God had delivered him from the pain-causing demon spirit.

With the service completed, the pastor gave me a check. I put it in my shirt pocket. As we were driving home, I handed the check to Linda. "What is the amount of the check?" I asked.

"Twenty dollars," she replied.

I commented, "Well, we broke even. I put $20 in the offering."

Linda smiled and said, "No, we didn't. We went in the hole. I put $5 in the offering!"

We paid our own expenses to drive one hundred miles to preach, purchase our own lunch, and donate $5 more than we were paid. What a memorable first time to preach!

But God had done a miracle in the service!

Obviously, God was in action and in full control of the ministry. It certainly was not me. I was only being obedient to Him.

A few weeks later, we went on a chartered bus trip to Stroud, Oklahoma. We were with about forty-five of the Native American congregation from the Cyril, Oklahoma, church. The Stroud church consisted of about one hundred to one hundred and fifty Black people. The bus driver, his wife, Linda, and I were the only "White" people at this church service. Six people were scheduled to preach that day. The service was advertised as "All Day Church with Dinner on the Ground." The fried chicken dinner eaten as we sat on the ground was delicious. It included several vegetables and tasty homemade pies.

When the pastor of the local "Black church" spoke, I noticed something unusual, something unique. I had never heard of this before. As the pastor spoke, a lady sitting three aisles from the front and to the right end of the pew would make encouraging remarks to him. She spoke loud enough that everybody could hear. She would make brief statements like, "Oh, that was good. Tell me more. Preach it, preach it. That is so good that I can hardly sit here," etc. She was very effective and influential to the pastor. The more the lady talked to the preacher, the stronger and more effective he preached. He began to speak in rhyme and swing his arms in rhythm.

After "Dinner on the Ground," we had a second session. I was the last speaker. It had been a long day. I noticed people were getting tired and restless. Instead of preaching my prepared sermon, I ministered from the gifts of the Holy Spirit to individuals. During the service, the Holy Spirit had given me messages for several of the audience. This type of ministry was new to this church. They received my ministry with obvious enthusiasm and excitement.

With the service completed, we boarded the bus for the 100-mile ride back to Cyril, then another 50-mile drive home. It had been a long day for Linda and me. I was excited to get to minister again. We learned much from the unusual day's trip and church service. God was teaching us in many different methods how He wanted us to minister.

Formal Ministry Training in Our Future

Over a period of time, thoughts and a desire to attend a Bible school began to develop in my mind. I discussed this with Linda. She was agreeable with the thoughts of her and I attending Bible school. Of course, Linda wanted to attend Bible school, also. She was in this spiritual change of life just as much as me. Natural logic told me that I needed to make inquiries as to where various Bible schools were located, the cost of attendance, what doctrinal teaching they emphasized, and all the other factors that might be involved in choosing a school.

I was generally familiar with Rhema Bible Center, Kenneth Hagin Ministries, located in Broken Arrow, Oklahoma. Thoughts of attending Rhema mixed among thoughts of attending elsewhere. During about two or possibly three weeks, this desire to attend Bible school became much stronger. My logical, though not necessarily spiritual, thoughts were that I could visit with local pastors of various denominations and gather all the information that I could about the schools of their denominations. For the schools I was most impressed with, I would contact them and get their enrollment literature for review. Through studying all this information, I could make an intelligent decision about which schools to contact for possible enrollment. My age of forty-seven was also an important factor to consider. This all seemed logical and reasonable to me.

The desire to attend Rhema became stronger by the day. Finally, I came to this conclusion: "I definitely want to attend Bible school and study evangelism. God had told me to 'go speak.' An evangelist 'goes' and speaks. A pastor 'stays' and speaks. I enjoy traveling, meeting new people, and being a positive influence on them. My personal style or manner of speaking seems more suitable to evangelism than pastoring. But where will I attend Bible school? I want to attend Rhema yet know little more about Rhema than any other Bible school."

One day, I happened to be visiting with a minister friend, Brosha. Linda and I had strong respect for Brosha and her knowledge of the Bible. She was the minister most sensitive in the spirit realm whom we were acquainted with at the time. After a very close forty-year friend-minister relationship, Brosha still fulfills those criteria. As I explained to Brosha my desire to attend a Bible school and the strongly increasing desire to attend Rhema, she strongly stated, "God does not want you to go to any other Bible school. He wants you to attend Rhema." I asked, "How do you know that?" Brosha coyly replied, "I asked God, and He told me." Brosha's comments settled the question of where to attend Bible school.

I discussed all this with Linda. Her desire had always been to attend Rhema, so we were in full agreement. We immediately started the long-involved process of preparing to move the two hundred miles to Broken Arrow, Oklahoma, and attend Rhema Bible Training Center.

When we announced this decision to family and friends, there came criticism. Close friends and relatives can hurt you the most. "What has gotten into Jerry? First, he says that God spoke to him in an audible voice and told him to go preach. Everybody knows that God does not speak to people in audible voices! Now, he is going to close his successful steel-building construction business, move his family two hundred miles away, and go to Bible school. Jerry is forty-seven years old. Look what age he will be when he finishes school: forty-nine years old. Jerry already has two degrees. Why does he want another degree, especially at his age? Forty-nine is too old to start a new career. If God wanted Jerry to preach, He would have called him when he was young. I have known Jerry for years. I know what he is like. He should not be a preacher. It just doesn't make a bit of sense!" On and on went the criticism. But I knew that I had heard from God. Linda was in full agreement with me. We were going to be obedient to God! Our applications to Rhema were accepted. We began to make plans to move.

Phase 2
Attending Rhema Bible Training College

Making the Move

Linda had accepted my call into the ministry as her call, also. We were in complete agreement concerning both of us being called into the ministry by God. The ministry was not a decision that she or I made independently without consideration of the other!

The next question was, "How are the circumstances going to work out?" Rhema was two hundred miles away, and I was in the steel-building construction business. Linda was under contract teaching school, and we had three children at home, ages nine, eleven, and thirteen.

During the next ten months, I brought the business to a close, selling the business equipment. Linda resigned from her teaching position. We openly discussed the move with the children. When looking for a house near the Rhema campus, Linda was out of town. The three kids and I found a house that fit our criteria and rented it. Much prayer was involved in the house search. Linda loved the house. Our prayers were answered.

We had a fourteen-foot by eighty-foot mobile home that had served us well for several years. Among the topics of severe criticism from various "friends" was, "Jerry and Linda will never be able to sell their mobile home. The gas-drilling boom has busted in Western Oklahoma. The local economy is falling fast. The newspaper is full of mobile homes for sale. What makes them think they can sell theirs? Their asking price is too high anyway." We prayed. The mobile home sold in very few weeks at our asking price. The local newspaper publisher, a friend of ours, made this comment: "Jerry and Linda must be doing something right. Their mobile home sold in three weeks. Other mobile homes have been advertised in our paper for three months at low prices and have not sold."

I have heard preachers say that the ministry is 10 to 20 percent spiritual and 80 to 90 percent natural or physical. At Rhema, it was emphasized that ministry is spelled w-o-r-k! Whether or not the stated percentages are accurate, it seems the physical, natural work takes far more time and effort than what we consider to be spiritual matters. Praying and consistent Bible study are only part of the spiritual time involved. When attending formal church services, counseling, traveling, and the myriad other responsibilities involved in ministry, it is often difficult to separate what is spiritual and what is natural. As an example, within the calling of an evangelist, I do a lot of traveling. As I travel, I pray and commune with God, Jesus, and the Holy Spirit. How does a person separate praying when driving or flying? It seems to be both spiritual and natural or physical at the same time. Somehow, it seems to blend.

During one driving trip, I checked in at a hotel overnight. This all seemed quite natural. During the business and conversation of checking in, I began to share the good news of Jesus with the young lady reservationist. Within just a few minutes, she received the baptism of the Holy Spirit and began praying in tongues, a new language. So, how much is spiritual, and how much is natural? I don't really know. I don't know that it really matters. I just do what God has called me to do: "You shall go speak. You shall speak to one or two, four or five, a hundred or two hundred, a thousand or more." It is always exciting to see Him work through me as I step out in faith.

So here we were at Rhema Bible Training College, located in Broken Arrow, a suburb of Tulsa, Oklahoma. The day after the move was completed, I left for San Francisco, California, to attend my second full weeklong motivational seminar. This seminar was titled "Empowerment." Only people who had completed the six-day motivational seminar presented by the same organization were eligible to attend. My brother, Ray, from Nashville, Tennessee, was also in attendance. He and I planned to have an exceptionally worthwhile experience. There were no restraints on what might be achieved within the guidelines set forth by the trainers. As the week's meeting progressed, eye-popping, mind-boggling thoughts began to come forth. The restrictive canopy-covering possibilities that had been created in my mind throughout my lifetime were being gradually eliminated. I began to realize that, truly, all things are possible. All I had to do was go make it happen. How does a person "go make it happen"? You start with nothing and end up with something! The example of a painter was given. The painter starts with a blank canvas. He begins to put marks of various colors and shapes on the canvas. Eventually, the painter creates a picture or painting. His work is creative in nature. He has started with nothing and ends up with something. In the process, he has used some knowledge, skills, and experience. But he was free to create, to make something new and different. There were no restraints to hold him back, to keep him from creating something new and different. He was free to create!

As I considered the book of Genesis Chapter 1, I noticed that in the account of the re-creation of the earth, in effect, God started with "nothing." "In the beginning God created the heavens and the earth. And the earth was formless and desolate emptiness, and darkness was over the surface of the deep, and the Spirit of God was moving over the surface of the waters" (Genesis 1:1–2, NASB). Then God spoke and followed with action. Everything that He wanted, He created by first speaking and then taking action. In this manner, He created the land with mountains, rivers, plants, and trees. He created the fish, birds, and eventually His supreme creation—man. God blessed what He had created; that is, He reviewed and approved of what He had accomplished. He saw that it was *good*. "And God saw all that He had made, and behold, it was very good. And there was evening and there was morning, the sixth day" (Genesis 1:31, NASB). Then God set aside His work and rested.

To "make things happen," I realized that I must follow God's example. How do I do that? The restraints in my thinking had been eliminated. Truly, God had spoken to me in a clear, distinct, and audible voice and appointed me as one of His representatives. Now, all I had to do was follow His example and continually communicate with Him about what to do and how to do it. That sounds simple. But time, effort, expenses, and a myriad of unknown and unexpected obstacles must be overcome. This takes time, much time. Time is a factor that is hardly ever addressed from the pulpit. Achieving a goal takes time, but "all things are possible with God" (Mark 10:27, NASB). "And Jesus said to him, 'If you can! All things are possible to him who believes'" (Mark 9:23, NASB).

When I returned to our new home in Broken Arrow, I was on a cloud. But the harsh reality of daily life, including the responsibility of being a husband and father, began to set in. *Where was the cloud that I had ridden home on?*

While I was gone, Linda had a fender bender in the car. Although the front end was mangled, minor repairs made the car operational. It just looked bad. We could drive the car and forego expensive body repairs. The car she ran into, which had stopped in the middle of the county road, made a fast getaway, never to be seen by her again.

I needed to find a job that would work with my class schedule at Rhema and allow study time.

Linda needed a job. The three teenagers still at home needed to be enrolled in new schools. Transportation for them needed to be arranged. School clothes needed to be shopped for and purchased. What seemed like an overwhelming multitude of other responsibilities were facing us. Pray, pray, pray. Hear from God and be obedient to what He tells us, even if it seems strange and unusual. Do what you need to do in the natural as well as the spiritual. Remember, "For all things are possible with God" (Mark 10:27, NASB).

It was and still is very important for Linda and me to communicate concerning various situations, come to an agreement, and then take action concerning our decisions. We also made a habit of communicating with the kids and considering their input concerning decisions that affected them. This helped develop their maturity and eliminated many possible problems, conflicts, and emotional upsets. It also promoted peace and harmony in our family relationships. So, daily, we made decisions and took actions that helped achieve our goal of learning all we could while attending Rhema. We were following the principle from the scripture in Isaiah 28:10 (NASB), "For He says, 'Order on order, order on order, line on line, line on line, a little here, a little there.'" Step by step, we were taking care of each and every responsibility to accomplish our goals. Classes at Rhema had not started yet. Still, a plan must be made and a foundation laid so we have something to build on and can accomplish our goals.

One afternoon, I was out jogging across the Rhema campus. One area of the campus that I particularly enjoyed spending time in was Rhema Park. The park had big shade trees, a small creek, a pond, picnic benches, and many ducks waddling around or swimming in the creek or pond. The park was very pleasant, peaceful, and enjoyable to spend time in. As I stepped across the sidewalk into the park, I could always sense the anointing of the Holy Spirit. Many other students made similar comments about the park. It was common for students to walk through the park or sit at a picnic bench and pray, read their Bibles, or just enjoy the peace and solitude of the park.

On this particular day, I visited with an older lady I quickly perceived to be very scripturally knowledgeable and spiritually mature. After a brief and pleasant visit, I jogged the two blocks home. I told Linda about the conversation with the lady. Linda commented, "I am surprised you did not invite her home for dinner."

My chivalrous and safe reply was, "I seriously considered that but thought I should talk to you before inviting a woman stranger to our home for dinner."

I jogged the two blocks back to the park. "Pat" was still at the picnic table, reading her Bible. She graciously accepted my invitation to dinner. We had a pleasant visit during the meal. As dinner was completing, the conversation turned to spiritual matters. Pat made this statement: "The Lord told me to tell you this, 'Be strong and courageous because you will lead a nation to Christ.'"

Linda and I both were overwhelmed and shocked. I courteously asked, "Are you sure that you are hearing from God? That is a powerful statement! After all, I am an unknown minister who has not even been to Bible school. I am just a small-town Okie who has been Spirit-filled only two years."

Pat replied with certainty and assurance, "I definitely have heard from God. I know the voice of God, and He clearly told me to give you this message. So you be strong and courageous, for you will lead a nation to Christ."

At an appropriate time, Pat excused herself and left our home. Linda and I discussed this visit and the prophecy from the new acquaintance. We were astonished at such a prophetic message. I thought, *Bible school classes have not even started, and God sends me such a powerful, life-changing message. What is coming next?*

After a couple of weeks, I wanted to visit with Pat again but had not seen her on campus. As I inquired with the dean of students, he informed me that the lady I described, "for personal reasons and circumstances, has chosen not to attend Rhema and returned to her home in the Phoenix, Arizona, area."

For legal privacy reasons, the dean could not give me her address. We have never had contact with the lady since that day. I occasionally wonder, *Was Pat a real human, or did we have a visitation from an angel in human form?* Hmmm, I have had similar experiences through the years that aroused this curious question.

One of the "problems" that we consistently had while living in the Tulsa area and attending Bible school was, "Which of the nationally or internationally known Christian full-gospel ministers will we go listen to this week?" Occasionally, there would be two or three in town the same night. In February 1985, that first year attending Rhema, we chose to attend a dinner meeting. Nora Lam, the Chinese-American missionary evangelist, was the honored speaker. For several years, Nora Lam had taken one hundred to three hundred people with her on mission trips to various countries of Asia, primarily China and the Philippines. From July to August 1985, she had scheduled a three-week mission trip to Taiwan, Hong Kong, Canton (in Communist China), and Manila, Philippines, and three days of R & R in Honolulu, Hawaii. When the meal ended, Nora Lam began to speak about mission evangelism and the planned trip to China. After a fifteen-to-twenty-minute presentation, she began to minister individually to various people by inspiration of the Holy Spirit. After speaking directly into people's lives through various gifts of the Holy Spirit, Nora pointed to Linda and me and asked us to stand up. Her statements to us were, "This summer, you will go to China on the mission trip with me. You be strong and courageous, for you will lead a nation to Christ."

There it was again, the same message, this time from a very well, internationally-known missionary evangelist. Nora Lam spoke this message quite boldly before the entire audience of at least two hundred people. Linda and I sat down, realizing the message from Nora Lam was exactly the same as the one given to us approximately six months previously in our home by Pat, our new lady acquaintance. Again, our minds were overwhelmed by this message and its confirmation of the previous message.

My thoughts were, *Who are we that God would choose to use us in such an extraordinarily powerful, far-reaching, responsible assignment? We are just small-town Okies. I am still in my first year of Bible school, and Linda hasn't even enrolled yet. She is working full-time to support me and the kids.*

Later, I prayed, "God, this is a tall order. I know nothing of how to lead a nation to Christ. I have led only a few individuals to Christ. But, God, if this is what You want me to do, certainly, I will do it. But I have no idea how, nor what country, nor when. You will have to totally guide and direct me. God, it is encouraging and inspirational to receive this same message from two different people, but this is such a great responsibility I need to hear directly from You."

The next day, Friday afternoon, after Rhema classes, I sat down at the kitchen table and worked out a budget for the trip to China. Including home expenses, our three young teenagers being taken care of, and the ministry trip expenses for three weeks around the world, the budget totaled $9,000. At the time, we were struggling to pay the monthly bills. Some of them were not being paid on time. So how were we to raise $9,000 in five months when we were desperately struggling to pay monthly living expenses? We had no knowledge or experience in raising money.

Pray! Pray! Pray! Do all that you know to do in the natural. Call upon God for the supernatural. Linda and I spent much, much time calling upon God for His supernatural provision. Through a combination of supernatural circumstances, the $9,000 came in. At 10:00 p.m., the night before we left, the last $80 was given to us.

Additional money was given to us by a trip member when we ran completely out of money the first week: "My wife has been praying for you, and God told her that you needed expense money." Another entire book could be written chronicling how the money was raised and the exciting, life-changing events of the three-week trip.

Anytime you commit to a mission trip, obstacles will arise. Sometimes, the obstacles will be severe enough to force a person to cancel the trip. Throughout the nine months between commitment and trip travel, many very troublesome obstacles arose. But Linda and I were committed. We overcame the smaller, less-troublesome obstacles. The following situation may indicate the strength of our commitment.

I had contracted to custom design and build a calf barn about two hundred miles from home. I was there working. Linda called and said she had a call from Nora Lam Ministries. It was a reminder that a large percentage of the trip expense money was due in five days. "We need to pay $1,500 to the ministry, and we have only $300 in our account for the trip. What are we going to do?"

My reply was, "Linda, we have plans to go to China with Nora Lam. We are committed! Let's stay with our plans. There is no plan B! We are going to China! The money will come in!" After lots of very serious prayer and some creative thinking, we managed to pay the $1,500 on schedule.

Obstacles

About three or four months after the trip commitment, I was discussing the situation on the phone with my brother, Ray. He and his wife lived in Atlanta, Georgia, eight hundred miles from our home. They asked if they could keep our three younger kids while we were gone to China. The kids were excited about that plan. We would drive the kids to Atlanta and then fly from Atlanta to San Francisco, California, where the entire mission group of two hundred and eighty-five people would assemble for the flight to Taiwan. Seven days before departure, Ray called and very apologetically explained, "We are having some very serious, unexpected problems here. We cannot keep your kids during the trip. Can you arrange something else for them?"

Man of great faith, like I wanted to think I was, I replied, "That is okay. Don't worry about it. We will find someone here locally to keep the kids." We had seven days to find someone to keep our three kids for three weeks at their expense.

Some of our "well-meaning" Christian friends made comments like this: "Oh, that is such a shame. You will never be able to find someone to keep your kids in only one week. Now you can't go to China."

Pray, pray, pray. Brosha and Ray Gattenby, our longtime ministry friends, offered to keep the kids. They lived close to the shore of Lake Eufaula. The kids could fish and swim and have an enjoyable time. This worked out well.

A Second Serious Obstacle

To earn a little more income before leaving on the trip, five days before leaving, I took a temporary minimum-wage job. We were installing a steel catwalk about ten feet high in a warehouse. I stepped on a piece of catwalk that had not been welded in place. It flipped, and I fell ten feet to a concrete floor, breaking bones in my left foot. After emergency hospital care, I was released to go home. The foot was swelling fast, so it was wrapped in an elastic bandage, no cast. Pain pills and an extremely painfully sensitive foot made walking on crutches very precarious and unstable. I spent the next three days in bed taking pain pills, barely coherent.

Again, some of our well-meaning, sympathetic Christian friends made comments like, "Oh, what a severe tragedy. Jerry broke his foot. He can't go to China on that mission trip now!"

Linda and I discussed the situation. We agreed. God wanted both of us to go to China. He did not say, "Don't go to China if you break your foot." I could walk on crutches. We were going to China! While riding in a car or on the plane, I rested my foot on a six-inch foam rubber pad. The foam pad absorbed mild vibration and kept my foot free of pain. Eight days later, Linda and a seamstress on the trip removed the eight stitches from cuts on the foot. The seamstress was familiar with "thread knots" and knew how to untie them. We completed the trip, the first of eventually thirty-five mission trips.

To accomplish God's work, we must overcome obstacles, sometimes severe, life-threatening obstacles. But you must pray, pray, and pray some more. Then do what you understand God wants you to do, or at least do what you think is best.

For continuity of our story, let's move on to the three days of R & R in Honolulu, Hawaii, that were scheduled as trip completion.

At that time in my life, I always slept throughout the entire night. Very, very seldom did I awake during the night. The first night in Honolulu, I awoke bright and alert at 3:00 a.m. I lay there close to an hour, wondering why I was so wide awake. Finally, with my "lightning-fast mind," the thought came to me: "Maybe God wants to talk to me." I asked, "God, is there something that You want to tell me?"

God does not mince words. His explicit response was, "Yes. Read My Book."

"Okay, God, I will read Your Book." So I quickly turned on the bedside lamp and opened my Bible. "Okay, God, where do You want me to read?"

His reply was, "Read My Book!"

"God, Your Book is quite lengthy, with sixty-six individual books within it. Where do You want me to read?"

"Read My Book!"

"Okay, God, I finally understand. I will read Your Book." Not knowing what better to do, I opened my Bible to Genesis Chapter 1. I skimmed through the pages, reading everything that I had previously highlighted or underlined. Often, I would also read parts not highlighted just to get the gist of the stories or accounts in each book. It was all good and interesting material, but nothing caught my attention until I reached the book of Isaiah. As I gleaned the highlights of Isaiah, I noticed my concentration becoming stronger and stronger. When I reached Isaiah 55:4–5, these verses seemed to be in big, bold, black letters, one-half inch above the page:

> *Behold, I have made him a witness to the peoples, a leader and commander for the peoples. Behold, you will call a nation you do not know, and a nation which does not know you will run to you, because of the LORD your God, the Holy One of Israel; for He has glorified you.*
>
> — Isaiah 55:4–5 (NASB)

There it was. God had awakened me in the middle of the night and given me the same message that the two individuals had given me. I skimmed through some of the rest of the Bible, but nothing caught my attention. So I closed the Bible, turned out the light, and immediately went sound asleep. During all of this, Linda slept soundly.

The second night, I awoke again at 3:00 a.m. sharp. I asked God, "Is there something You want to tell me, God?"

His reply was, "Read My Book."

Again, I skimmed through the highlights. As I reached the middle of the book of Isaiah, again, my concentration became stronger and stronger. Isaiah 55:4–5 were powerfully strong, but not like the first night. I turned the page, and Chapter 58:6–12 seemed to jump off the page in big, bold, black letters. These seemed to be details of what and how events would develop as I led a nation to Christ. After reviewing these scriptures closely, I seemed comfortable that God's message on this second night was complete. I closed the Bible, turned out the light, and quickly went into a sound sleep. Linda kept snoozing.

Night three, 3:00 a.m. I was wide awake, so I turned on the lamp and opened my Bible. "God, do You have another message for me?"

"Read My Book."

Once more, I opened to Genesis and skimmed through the Bible, reading the highlights. Once more, my concentration became strong in the latter chapters of Isaiah. The verses in chapters 55 and 58 were still powerful. As I turned the pages, Chapter 60:1–3 seemed to rise off the page in big, bold, black letters.

> *Arise, shine; for your light has come, and the glory of the LORD has risen upon you. For behold, darkness will cover the earth and deep darkness the peoples; but the LORD will rise upon you, and His glory will appear upon you. Nations will come to your light, and kings to the brightness of your rising.*
>
> — Isaiah 60:1–3 (NASB)

Three nights in a row, God had awakened me at 3:00 a.m. sharp and spoke to me through His written Word. Yes, I will lead a nation to Christ. God had spoken to me through a spiritually strong individual who was relatively unknown in the ministry. He had spoken the same message to me through a spiritually strong, internationally well-known minister. Now, He had spoken to me through His written Word and confirmed the first two messages. Although still overwhelmed with the task and its tremendous responsibility, I was at peace with and assured of the assignment. My immediate questions were, "What country is it? When will it happen? How will it happen?"

Since these messages were spoken to me in 1984 and 1985, Linda and I both have graduated from Rhema Bible Training College. We pastored a church for three years, and we have done the work of the ministry as evangelists for thirty-seven years. We have been to sixteen countries on thirty-five mission trips, plus evangelizing from Maine to California. Each trip, I ask God, "Is this the country that I am to lead to Christ?" He has not answered me clearly and distinctly. But during the past sixteen years, events have happened that indicate the country it may be. Time and circumstances will tell. I suspect that after everything has taken place, and the results are common knowledge, I will look back over time and circumstances and be able to say, "This is the country! This is where and how God used Linda and me. As we did the works of Jesus, always guided by His Holy Spirit, God used us to lead a nation to Christ."

What a way to start Bible school! What was going to happen during the rest of our time at Rhema?

When I enrolled at Rhema, I was forty-seven years old. The criticism and ridicule from family, friends, and the "Christian community" with whom we were formerly associated was severe. Many of these people separated themselves from us, making comments like, "Ole good time, let's have a party, Jerry" has gone off the deep end on religion. He even has Linda and the kids mixed up in that religious stuff, too. It doesn't make a bit of sense. Why is he going back to school anyway? He already has a bachelor's degree and a master's degree. He is forty-seven years old. Look how old he will be when he graduates, almost fifty years old! He is all mixed up and making a mess of his life. He just doesn't make sense at all."

These were just a few of the harsh critical comments I'd heard. What else was said is probably best I did not hear. I knew I had heard from God. He had spoken to me in a clear, distinct, and audible voice and told me to "go speak." Whatever the criticism and obstacles, I was going to be obedient to Him!

Time at Rhema!

Wow! How do you describe two years of daily mountaintop experiences? Day after day, each and every class could be compared to the best, most worthwhile, and most effective church services I had ever attended. Often, I sat in class spellbound. Other students were avidly taking notes from the consistent, outstanding teaching. But there I sat, class after class, absorbing all I could, wanting to remember every detail so I could use this material in future preaching-teaching. Yes, I took some notes. When reviewed, they put me right back in class, learning again and being spiritually refreshed by each superb teaching.

During the forty class subjects we studied within the two years, there were instructors who influenced me more favorably than others. I found very few difficult to listen to because of their style of presentation. What they taught was very worthwhile. One instructor, to me, was dry and boring. Another instructor was arrogant and self-centered. A third instructor did a lot of emotional preaching and very little teaching. Each one of these instructors had twenty to fifty years of ministry experience. They had pastored churches and served as evangelists or teachers. Each was obviously anointed by the Holy

Spirit. I just did not like their style of presentation. So I had to make a decision. Would I shut them out because of my likes and dislikes, or would I learn from them? Common-sense wisdom told me to discipline myself and learn from the different styles of presentation. Each instructor was teaching out of his own personality, bodily emotions, experiences, and whatever else inspired him to teach in his particular manner. I needed to develop my own style of presentation. It should not be a copy of any other speaker. How and what could I present that would be accepted by an audience and influence them? I had so much to learn. It was apparent that I could learn from what I considered to be negative as well as what I considered to be positive. I made the decision to develop my own style of presentation and not copy even those I admired the most. Using my body, my voice, and my personality, I would work at developing a style of presentation that would be receptive, effective, and worthwhile for whatever particular audience I was speaking to. A frank appraisal of comments from individuals after a presentation, plus audience reaction while you are speaking, helps the speaker evaluate his effectiveness.

As an example, I received an invitation to speak to a Christian school's upper elementary age group. There were possibly two hundred students in the audience. My youngest daughter, a sixth-grader, was present. All her young life, she had been known for speaking frank, honest truth as she understood it. I was a second-year Rhema Bible Training College student "full of the good Word of God." I had prepared a teaching that surely would appeal and be worthwhile to this particular audience. Everything seemed to go well. At home that evening, I asked my daughter, "What did you think of my teaching today?"

She replied, "It was okay, but what was your point?" Back to square one. Start all over again.

As well as learning the biblical material taught, I began to study each instructor. What did they do to be scripturally prepared? How much time was spent in prayer? How much time did each of them apparently spend in Bible study and lesson preparation? How did they know what to say, what and when to do? How did they keep the audience's attention? How did they get their points across? Did they consciously use body mannerisms and posture? What and how could I learn from the physical presentation of each of these instructors? How could I incorporate all I was learning into a style of presentation that would be "right" for me?

In the past, I had taught school and coached football for twelve years. I studied the subject of communication so I could more effectively communicate with my football players. The purpose and goal were to win football games. I thought, due to this experience, that I was knowledgeable concerning communicating with an audience. *Wrong!* Often, the church audience response indicated that I had far more to learn than I already knew. I must eliminate my ego and go back to the basics of communication. Learn from both the positive and the negative. "Humble yourselves in the presence of the Lord, and He will exalt you" (James 4:10, NASB). Am I willing to humble myself before people? Am I humble or arrogant? There were many lessons to be learned while attending Rhema in addition to the scriptural teaching.

Among the many outstanding, life-changing subjects taught at Rhema by the superbly prepared and Holy Spirit-anointed instructors was "Submission and Authority," taught by Keith Moore. Every lesson spoke directly to me. I began to develop a far-clearer understanding of when, where, why, and how to submit, as well as to take authority in various situations. Under what conditions and before whom do you submit or take authority? All this blends in with plans, purpose, conditions, circumstances, and your own motivational gifts and personality. No doubt there are many other factors to consider. As I have studied the life of Jesus, I noticed that He was a strong individual, that He made the choices, the decision of when, where, before whom, and in what conditions He would submit Himself or take authority. To be like Jesus, I must develop in all areas of my life: spirit, soul, and body. This development is a lifelong process. I have much to learn! As was continually emphasized at Rhema, what we learned, what was taught there, was only a foundation for what we needed to know to effectively do the work of the ministry.

One evaluation I made concerning the superior quality of Bible teaching at Rhema was the following: if I thought back through the years and recalled the best sermons I had ever heard from various preachers, each and every class was equivalent to those best sermons. Most of the classes were superior to those sermons. Many days, I would be on such a "spiritual high" that I could not recall walking across campus and the three additional blocks home. I wondered sometimes if I floated home on a cloud or, like Philip as recorded in Acts 8:39–40, was snatched away and found myself at home.

In addition to class reading assignments, I was often inspired to do independent studies in the Bible. One such study was "Healing, as Performed by Jesus." I searched through the Gospels of Matthew, Mark, Luke, and John. I located every scripture where Jesus healed someone or cast out demons. I noticed that, often, a disease or crippling condition was caused by a demon spirit in a person. The demon from hell was the cause of the disease or crippling condition. When Jesus cast the demon out of the person, the healing would take place. The following principle became prominent with me: determine the cause of a person's illness, minister to that cause, and the healing will take place.

As I studied how Jesus healed people, I noted all the conditions stated in the various accounts.

Was it a man, woman, or child? Was the person in a notable position of life or an unknown? What did Jesus say to the person? What did the person reply to Jesus? Were other people involved? Was faith in healing a contributing factor? Was faith in Jesus as the Messiah a strong factor? How much time was likely involved? I noticed that the statements of Jesus were simple, brief, and to the point. In each situation, there was no confusion or doubt about what He said. I like to state it this way: Jesus spoke with the pure, impeccable integrity of truth, and people were healed every time. There was never any confusion, doubt, apprehension, or fear in His statements. Jesus spoke pure truth, and miracles happened. Jesus never prayed and asked God to heal anyone. He merely spoke pure truth to people in need, and the healing took place.

Following Jesus's example, I changed my methods and techniques when dealing with a healing effort. I worked diligently at changing my speech patterns and habits. I eliminated any words or phrases that might create confusion or doubt in what I was saying or doing. I eliminated all fears, doubts, apprehensions, uneasiness, hesitation, and qualms from my speech. Needless to say, this took a lot of time and conscientious effort. But the results were well worth the time and effort. I quit praying and asking God to heal people! Rather, I began to minister healing to them. I began to speak pure, simple truth, and miracles of healing began to take place. I was no longer "trying to get people healed"; rather, I was ministering God's healing to people. After all, it is God who has the healing power, not me.

Most people are aware that the individual does not have the skill, knowledge, or supernatural power to heal people. It is God who does the healing. However, there are many things we can do that will build healing faith in the person who is diseased or crippled. As we do these things, the person needing the healing will more readily receive from both us and God. This statement of Jesus becomes a truth for them: "Daughter, take courage; your faith has made you well" (Matthew 9:22, NASB).

What else was I to learn while attending Rhema that was supplemental to the classroom teaching? At the time, I was not aware of the impact that these supplemental lessons would have on me as an individual and the ministry that God had called me into. Doing these studies just seemed like the thing to do.

One healing incident that caught my attention so strongly that I have never forgotten was this. Early one morning at home, my fifteen-year-old son, Paul, complained, "Dad, I have such a severe headache that I need to stay home from school." Without giving it much thought, I laid hands on Paul's head and spoke healing to him. I commanded the pain to leave Paul's head. Then I went on about the early morning activities. A few minutes later, Paul went with his sisters to school. That afternoon, I went to the school to get Paul and take him to a chiropractor. When Paul came into the school lobby, I told him what I wanted to do. He commented, "Dad, I don't have a headache. You prayed for me. Where is your faith?" This incident brought a boost to my faith. Paul received. God had healed him. His faith had made him well. My faith was increased also.

How do I describe the many surprising, shocking, and mind-boggling experiences and teachings that Linda and I received during the four years of attending Rhema? Each of these events or situations would in some way influence us in our daily lives then and in ministry work in future years. I have stated that Rhema, when we attended, was a two-year ministry training center.

Yet it took us four years to complete the schooling. The first year I attended class, in 1984–85, Linda taught fourth grade at Victory Christian School in nearby Tulsa, Oklahoma. Her job provided much-needed family financial income. The second year, we both worked. In the third year, we both attended classes at Rhema. Linda completed her first year. I completed my second year and graduated in May 1987. In the fourth year, I worked, and Linda completed her second year and graduated in May 1988. With three teenage children, Linda attending school, and me working when and as I could find work, finances were an extreme struggle. Our daughter Cheryl now had her driver's license. Due to driving to school, work, and church activities, she needed a car. We managed for Cheryl to buy a car and pay for it herself with the income from her part-time jobs. Paul went to work at a nearby McDonald's fast-food restaurant and did other part-time jobs. Janice was only thirteen and found it very difficult to enter the workforce. During the spring semester, Linda and I were both out of work. Desperate for income, she and I took the only job we could find, cleaning offices at night at very low wages. Fortunately, Linda was dependable and hardworking. Quite frankly, I hated the work. But we were desperate for the income. Some people might say that with a bachelor's degree and master's degree and within six weeks of completing Bible school, I was to learn humility from the experience. God was trying to teach me to be a servant. Nonsense! I hated the job and learned nothing except how to clean commodes, empty ashtrays, and clean an office fast. But thanks to Linda's insistence, we stayed with the job until I finally found something better.

It often seems that when a task is getting close to completion, obstacles and various difficulties arise that cause discouragement, frustration, doubt, and questions of worth. "It would be much easier to do something else. I am tired of this. Is it really necessary to complete this plan? I would rather do something that doesn't require so much time and effort every waking moment." These types of thoughts and questions are common when the going gets rough.

As the last semester at Rhema progressed, the "going" got rougher and tougher. Linda and I had to constantly remind ourselves that the goal of graduation was getting closer and closer. But the mountain we were climbing was getting steeper and steeper. The goal was at the peak of the mountain. We had crossed the valleys, streams, hills, and surrounding low mountains. This last mountain with the crown or goal on top was extremely rugged. With three teenagers to feed and to satisfy their growing appetites, plus Linda and me, it was a daily struggle to put meals on the table. In addition were the normal monthly expenses of house rent, car maintenance, gasoline, and all the normal costs of daily living for a family of five. Even today, some thirty-five years later, our children do not care for pots of stew or beans. I even have been guilty of putting a little extra water in those pots to make the food last longer. But we did have our low-paying office-cleaning jobs that were providing a subsistence income.

Completion of what we start has always been important to both Linda and me. We are not quitters! We had made the commitment to not only attend Rhema but also graduate.

Somehow, we would fulfill that commitment! Somehow, I had to provide income to pay for our living expenses and Linda's second year at Rhema. Food is a daily need for each and every person.

One day, my sister called and asked if I would help butcher a hog. Our father had owned and operated a slaughterhouse from the time I was nine to fourteen years old. Dad saw to it that each of us kids learned the slaughter butchering skills at a very young age. The labor we provided to the business was a help. Not having butchered since she was about twelve years old, some thirty-eight years ago, Nona called big brother Jerry for help.

As kids, when Dad needed to be gone for various business reasons, and there were cattle or hogs that needed to be butchered, we kids did the butchering. Ray's attitude then was, "Dad taught me to butcher when I was little. I am nine years old now. I know what and how to do it. If I don't know what to do, all I have to do is ask my big brother. He knows what to do and how to butcher. He is thirteen years old!"

One Saturday, Dad had to be gone on business. There were twenty-five hogs to be butchered that day. Dad told us, "You boys start early and butcher as many as you can. I will come home as early as possible and help you finish the twenty-five hogs. But it is critical that we butcher all twenty-five hogs today!" After an eight-hour workday, nine-year-old Ray and I had all twenty-five hogs butchered and in the cooler. The killing floor was cleaned. We were in the yard playing baseball when Dad drove in from the day's business trip.

At an early age, we had been taught to work hard and complete what we started. This lesson proved to be a strong asset as we were getting close to finishing school at Rhema.

By the time I arrived at Nona's house late that afternoon, she and her family had completed the butchering job. As they discussed where and how to properly dispose of the head, hide, and other waste, I offered to take the head home with me. Most people would have disposed of the head with the other waste, but I remembered an old recipe brought from Germany by my great-grandmother. I would make hog's head cheese. This would add a few much-needed meals to our table.

I disposed of the ears, eyeballs, snout, skin, and anything else that I did not want to eat. Next, I split the head into two pieces with a large cleaver used in the slaughterhouse for splitting cow or hog backbones. I put the two pieces of the hog's head into a large pot, covered them with water, and boiled the pieces for about twelve hours. The long boiling process cooked all the meat off the bone. The skull joints were all separated. The next step is to strain out all bones, teeth, and whatever else you don't want to or cannot eat. What is left is a thick broth with shredded meat and a gelatin substance from the bone. Add salt, pepper, sage, and any other spices that appeal to your taste. When the broth has an agreeable flavor, add a quantity of cornmeal to the broth to make it a thick gravy consistency. Pour this into small containers. I used two-inch by two-inch by six-inch pans. Chill in the refrigerator. The chilled cornmeal broth sets up to a consistency similar to cheese. The result is hog's head cheese.

After watching me prepare the hog's head, our teenagers would not even taste the "cheese." Linda and I decided it would make a tasty light lunch. We could sit in the car after morning classes and eat hog's head cheese and crackers before leaving for work to clean offices and toilets. The first week's lunch was enjoyable. The second week was okay. In the third week, we brought pickles or anything else we could find to break the daily lunch taste routine of "cheese and crackers." Three more weeks of school. Three more weeks of hog's head cheese and crackers. Oh no! Not again today! Regardless, however the cheese tasted by then, it still was better than missing lunch.

One day as we sat in the car "enjoying" lunch, we were discussing the overall situation. Needless to say, there had been much daily prayer, sometimes desperate prayer. God had reminded me of completion, reaching the goal. Drawing on my experience as a football coach, I realized that we were close to the goal line. We were in scoring territory. We score, we win! As I discussed this with Linda over another "tasty" lunch, we were clear that we would somehow reach our goal of completing that school term. I would graduate and then find a job that would provide sufficient income for her to attend the second year. Reviewing the football analogy, I pointed out that the team you are playing against is your opponent. They want to keep you from scoring so they can win. If your team has the ball in the open field, the opponent's defense is spread out. They have much of the field to cover. When you get within the ten-yard line, your team is within close scoring territory. The opposing team has far less territory to defend. They can amass their defenses into this small territory and fight hard to keep you from scoring, winning, or succeeding. This was the situation we were in. We were close to the goal line, in scoring territory. It seemed that Satan had amassed his demon forces against us to cause us to fail.

God and Satan are still fighting a spiritual war. We, as ministers, are God's representatives. In this analogy, we were His football players. The opponent, Satan, does not want God's representatives to be successful, to win. We reminded ourselves of scriptures such as 1 John 4:4 (NASB), "because greater is He who is in you than he who is in the world"; Revelation 12:11 (NASB), "And they overcame him by the blood of the Lamb and the word of their testimony"; Mark 9:23 (NASB), "And Jesus said to him, 'If you can! All things are possible to him who believes'"; and Matthew 19:26 (NASB), "And looking upon them Jesus said to them, 'With men this is impossible, but with God all things are possible.'"

We had the Spirit of the living God within us. We were overcomers. We would overcome our negative circumstances. We would reach our goal by the power of the living God operating in us. In that discussion, the analogy of being in scoring territory encouraged and inspired us. We would complete our goal! With a smile and grim determination, we took another bite of "cheese" and left to clean the toilets and offices one more time.

After graduation, we had full days free from classes. We managed to find full-time, better-paying jobs. The financial pressure was gradually being relieved. Linda enrolled for her second year at Rhema. We perceived the scriptural, spiritual training for both of us as inconceivably good. We were ready (or so we thought) for the full-time ministry. However, providing for family living expenses and Linda's last year at Rhema were facing us. As teenagers grow older, their school activities increase, and so do their appetites for food, plus other expenses. That fall, Linda's parents took our three teenagers shopping for school clothes and supplies. What a blessing they were to us!

That last year, we continued to take advantage of the training in church services and the weekly well-known and respected evangelists who ministered in various large Tulsa churches. Including Linda attending Rhema, our overall spiritual education continued.

Phase 3
Hospital Ministry

Ted's Story

One of my sisters, who at the time seriously doubted my ministry call, phoned me at about 7:15 one morning. She stated that a friend of her family had been in an automobile accident and was in a very serious life-death circumstance. He had been life-flighted about one hundred miles with "no expectancy to survive the flight." My sister asked if I would go to St. Francis Hospital in Tulsa, where he had been taken, and "do whatever it is you do" for him. I answered that after classes at Rhema and lunch (at home—before "cheese"), I would go visit "Ted" at the hospital. During the noon hour, she called again and said, "Jerry, I went to the hospital this morning. Ted has been unconscious since the accident three days ago. He is in extremely bad physical condition. He is on life support, and the doctors do not expect him to survive more than a few hours. I talked to his wife, Annie, in the waiting room. She is in such a severe emotional condition that she cannot even carry on a conversation. I would ask her questions, and all she would reply is, 'God is good. God will heal my husband. Isn't God wonderful?' And similar statements. Jerry, Ted is going to die at just any time. It would be a waste of time for you to drive to the hospital. I am sorry that I bothered you."

My reply to my doubting sister (Doubting Thomas?) was, "I have dealt with people in similar conditions before. After talking with Annie, I can determine if she is actually mentally and emotionally unbalanced. I will go to the hospital as soon as I finish lunch."

This was the beginning of one full year of ministering to people at St. Francis Hospital. As I ministered to someone, hospital visitors within hearing range would often ask me to go to another room and pray for someone else. At various people's requests, I ministered health and healing for one to five patients every trip to the hospital. I also ministered peace and encouragement to their families. This happened, by estimate, an average of five days per week for one full year. After one year, the invitations stopped. I did not seek nor go back to St. Francis Hospital in an attempt to generate more ministry opportunities. Approximately five years later, in a conversation with God, He clearly pointed out to me that this was Phase 3 of my training for the ministry.

Back to Ted and Annie.

When I arrived at St. Francis Hospital, the ICU waiting room was packed full of about forty people. *How do I determine which is Annie?* At the doorway, I called her name. A lady stood up. After introducing ourselves, Annie asked, "Are you a Spirit-filled minister?" I replied, "Yes, I am. I am still a student at Rhema Bible Training Center, but I am a Spirit-filled minister."

"Praise God, praise God," she exclaimed. "I have been here for three days praying that God would send a Spirit-filled minister to pray for my husband, Ted, and here you are. Oh! Praise God, praise God! He has answered my prayer!"

Annie spent about thirty minutes sharing details of the accident and their spiritual background. After hearing that information, I first ministered God's hope, encouragement, and faith to Annie. She obviously needed strengthening both spiritually and emotionally. With your spouse unconscious and in a critical life-death situation, anyone would need strengthening.

We went to Ted's ICU room. He lay on his bed breathing with the assistance of a life-support machine. His face was marred by cuts and scratches. Several ribs were broken. His spinal cord was severed in the lower back. His lungs and kidneys would not function without the life support machine. Only by the grace and love of God could this man recover.

In a situation like this, we must make a choice. As we view the circumstances, we must either accept what appears to be the inevitable outcome or call upon God for His supernatural power to intervene and overcome the natural physical circumstances. I chose to follow the scripture Deuteronomy 30:19 (NASB): "I have set before you life and death, blessings and cursings. Choose life that you may live." We would operate in faith! It clearly was going to take the power of God's Word and all our faith in speaking His Word to overcome Ted's physical circumstances.

We were in the best of hospitals with the best of doctors doing all that they knew to do medically and physically. It was the job of Annie and me to do all we knew to do spiritually. With her husband in this physical condition, I recognized that Annie, Ted's wife, was, of necessity, the spiritual leader in the husband-wife relationship. She freely gave me spiritual authority to operate however I saw necessary.

We anointed Ted with oil, laid hands on him, and spoke health, healing, and recovery to him. We then prayed and thanked God for Ted's recovery. Nothing happened that we could determine. But we were operating by faith, not by sight. I prayed with Annie and went home, telling her that I would be back the next day.

In these situations, I often do not know what to do in my natural mind. I spend much time talking to and listening to the Holy Spirit. Then, I do what He tells me or seems best to do. I constantly remind myself that I must operate with faith in God because I do not have the knowledge, power, or skill to heal anyone. It is God who will do the healing. All I do is speak His Word. God's power and authority are embodied in His Word. I speak God's Word in faith that He will perform His Word. *I speak (quote) God's Word!*

On the second day at the hospital, I followed a similar procedure. I shared God's Word with Annie to build a strong foundation of faith in her. I anointed Ted with oil, laid hands on him, and then spoke health, healing, and recovery to him as I had done the first day. Nothing happened that either of us could determine. After many days of no noticeable change to us, the doctors stated that Ted's vital signs were improving. Encouragement!

After about six weeks of daily ministering, it was obviously noticeable that Ted's abdomen was severely bloated. I asked Annie if his bowels were functioning. She said, "No. They have not worked since the accident." I replied, "If his bowels don't start working soon, he will die of intestinal poisoning!" This was a statement of physical fact. In my view, too many "faith preachers" are so adamant about never speaking "the negative" that they inadvertently neglect the physical facts of a situation. I see it necessary to deal with the physical facts of a situation in words and in action. Once those physical facts are determined, we can concentrate on the spiritual truths that apply to those facts and overcome the physical facts. But we must concentrate on the spiritual truth, always speaking God's Word in faith that God will perform His Word. Isaiah 55:11 (NASB) states, "So shall my word be which comes from my mouth; it will not return to me empty, without accomplishing what I desire and without succeeding in the matter for which I sent it."

The question comes up: "If we are truly going to operate in faith, should we use doctors, medicine, and hospitals?" Let us remember this: Luke, who wrote the Gospel of Luke and the book of Acts, was a physician. God used that doctor mightily. By that precedent, yes, we can use doctors and today's advanced medical procedures. The Amplified Bible in Proverbs 18:9 states, "He who does not use his endeavors to heal himself, is a brother to he who commits suicide." We should do everything that we know to do for our health and recovery from sickness or accidents. If you get a bad cut or break a bone, doesn't common sense tell you to go to a doctor and get the wound repaired? In the process, just remember that it is the doctor who does the repair work. It is God who does the healing.

Annie and I anointed Ted's abdomen with oil, laid hands on his abdomen, and commanded them to start working. Nothing that we could see happened. The next day, the same procedure. Same "apparent results." On the third day, in the waiting room, Annie told me, "Ted has been soiling the bed all day. His bowels are working!" Ted's bowels worked normally until he died a natural death nine years later at age seventy-four. Praise God for His healing power still working today.

The cause of Ted's injuries was that He had apparently dozed off to sleep, ran off the road, and hit a tree. He was driving the few miles to town from his farm. The emergency ambulance attendants thought that his injuries were so severe that he would not survive the fifteen-mile trip to McAlester. But he did. The emergency doctors in the local hospital said they were not equipped to handle the severity of his injuries. He would die in their hospital. The only hope was to life-flight him the one hundred miles to Tulsa. "With the severity of his injuries, he is not likely to survive the flight." But he did. Annie told me that she had recently been baptized in the Holy Spirit. "All that I knew to do was pray in faith and not speak the negative." Annie had been praying with all the faith that she had, and she certainly was not going to "speak the negative." What she was doing and saying in the waiting room, my sister did not understand. My sister was a logical thinker. To her way of thinking, Annie was not a bit logical. "Her husband was severely injured and dying, and all she can do is tell you how good God is. She doesn't make a bit of sense."

With the damage to the chest from the steering wheel, Ted's lungs were not functioning. There was also a bad infection in the lung cavity. At one point, the doctors drained four quarts of blood, pus, and water from his chest cavity. Gradually, Ted was improving. He was in and out of consciousness. Finally, Ted stayed conscious. Improving health was obvious. The doctors kept doing what they knew to do. Annie and I kept doing what we knew to do. Three months after the accident, Ted was transferred to the rehabilitation section of the hospital. After two months of rehab, he was sent home fully recovered, except that he could not walk.

Agreement of the patient with the minister is critical to recovery. Many times, Jesus told people, "Your faith has made you well." They agreed and believed that Jesus could heal them. I have found in the New Testament that after He was resurrected, Jesus told His disciples, "All authority in heaven and earth has been given to me" (Matthew 28:18, NASB). Mark recorded in his Gospel, "In my name they will cast out demons, they will speak with new tongues; they will pick up serpents, if they drink any deadly poison, it shall not hurt them; they will lay hands on the sick and they shall recover" (Mark 16:17, 18, NASB). Christians are today's disciples of Jesus. He gave us "Power of Attorney" to use His authority and do these supernatural things, if we will use His name.

I was able to persuade Ted that he could and would recover from every injury except the severed spinal cord. Even though he had some feeling (nerve function) in his feet and legs, because of the severed spinal cord diagnosis, Ted believed he would never be able to walk. He never did walk during the remaining nine years of his life. The principle in Proverbs 23:7 (NASB) became a truth and reality for Ted. "As you believe within yourself, so are you."

Ted had special controls mounted on his bed so he could move himself into his wheelchair. He also had special controls mounted in his new pickup truck that enabled him to drive. Now, he could drive himself the few miles to his farm ranch and oversee the work being done by employees.

Ted became the teacher of the men's class at his church. With ample time available, he bought reference books, charts, and Bible area maps to study and teach with. The collection of quality study-teaching materials that he showed me in his home made me envious. Soon, his class of five men grew to forty members. He obviously was serious and dedicated to his teaching efforts. Ted also expressed his appreciation to God for his recovery. Ted accomplished all these things after being near death and unconscious for six weeks. The power of God's Word instilled in him during the five-month recovery period made a definite impact on his life. The biblical definition of recovery as used in Mark 16:18 (NASB), is "healing over a process of time." Ted had recovered!

The primary lesson for me in these ministry circumstances was that God's Word works! God is still healing people today if we will accept and apply the truth of His Word to our circumstances.

Nellie's Story

One day in the hospital ICU waiting room, I happened to be sitting close to the pay phone that was attached to a wall. A lady was talking to someone about her thirty-two-year-old daughter, who was unconscious and at the point of death. After her phone conversation was complete, I introduced myself and asked if I could be of assistance as a minister. She seemed desperate with her "Yes" reply. I questioned the lady concerning the details of her daughter's circumstances. Her story went like this: "For about five days, my daughter seemed discouraged, and then one day, she was very despondent. The next day, she lapsed into a coma. She was taken to St. Francis Hospital by ambulance. After many tests, the doctors could find nothing physically wrong with her. Yet, 'Nellie' was getting weaker each day. After sixteen days, the doctors were dumbfounded and were offering no hope for her recovery. They indicated a possibility of twenty-four hours of life at the current rate of declining weakness."

I asked the mother, "Has Nellie been prayed for?"

"Oh yes. We are Spirit-filled Christians. Her husband, father, and I have prayed for her. Our pastor and other members of the church have prayed for her. But the prayers and doctors' care have not helped."

I asked, "May I pray for her?"

She urgently responded, "Yes, yes."

I said, "I want to go into her ICU room alone. May I do that?"

"Yes, go ahead."

The scripture in 1 Corinthians 11:30 (NASB) states this, "For this reason, many among you are weak and sick and a number are asleep [died]." Some time ago, as I studied that scripture, this thought strongly came to me: *Determine the "reason or cause," minister to the cause or reason of sickness, and the healing will take place.* With Nellie, the "cause" had not been recognized and ministered to. I suspected the overlooked cause of her rapidly declining strength and health. Every area had been ministered to medically and spiritually, except demon possession. I suspected that demons were killing her. As I stepped through the doorway of the ICU room, I thought, *Mercy me, this room is full of demons! It is demons that are killing Nellie.*

DEMONS

What are demons? What is the origin of demons? What is the purpose of their existence? Demons and their activities are often mentioned in the Bible, especially in the New Testament. Many Christian books describe their activities and purposes. Comparatively, little is taught in these books about the origin of demons. After doing meticulous and exhaustive research concerning their origin, I concluded that the former archangel Lucifer (Satan, the devil) used his superior powers and created demons as his messengers to fight against God and His faithful creation. The creation of demons was done after Lucifer was cast down to earth (Isaiah 14:12). The rebellious angels were "cast into the darkness of hell and kept in chains until their judgment day" (2 Peter 2:4 and Jude 6, NASB). The purpose of demons is to perform the will of the devil and cause harm, even death, to mankind. Demons seem to have the character and nature of their creator "to steal, kill and destroy" (John 10:10, NASB).

A DEMON-POSSESSED "WITCH DOCTOR" EXPERIENCE

During one of eleven mission trips to Zimbabwe, I was scheduled to speak at a ministry conference in the capital city of Harare. A few minutes before the first scheduled speaker, a local lady approached me with a request. "My husband's family doesn't like me, and they have our village witch doctor casting spells on me. He is causing me all kinds of problems. Pray for me? Do something!?" Being the only "White" man there, this lady recognized me as an American missionary. How was I going to handle this?

This young lady was obviously in a serious, fearful, and stressful situation. She explained to me that the witch doctor might use his (demon-spiritual) powers to kill her. Fortunately,

I had previously had some biblical teachings about demons and spiritual warfare. Ephesians 6:17 (NASB) states, "[T]he sword of the Spirit, which is the word of God." I began to use the Word of God as a weapon to fight this spiritual battle. That witch doctor knew the source of his spiritual power and was using it. I relied on the truth of God's Word and its spiritual power and was using it. I was confident in my knowledge of God's Word. Jesus is quoted in Matthew 28:18 (NASB) saying, "All authority has been given to Me in heaven and on earth." In Mark 16:17 (NASB), Jesus is quoted saying, "[I]n My name they will cast out demons." Jesus has given Christians the Power of Attorney to use His name. I used the name of Jesus and quoted scripture to break the spiritual power of that witch doctor. The lady thanked me and left, saying, "I cannot stay for the conference. If my husband's family finds out I am here, I will be in even worse trouble."

I was the third scheduled speaker that morning. After the few minutes of praise and worship singing between speakers, I stepped behind the speakers' podium. Glancing across the crowd, I saw the lady I had ministered to sitting in a backseat. She had tears of joy on her face and, with her hands raised high, was praising God wholeheartedly. She stayed for the conference and worshiped God all morning. The demonic witch doctor inspired spiritual power with its fear had been effectively removed from her.

BACK TO NELLIE

Let's go back to the hospital. I took the attitude of a heavyweight boxing champion of the world. At that moment, in his prime, former world boxing champion Muhammed Ali could not top me in attitude and comments. One big difference was that Muhammed Ali bragged about himself to glorify himself. Then, he used "trash talk" to discourage and degrade his opponent.

I quoted scripture that glorified God and Jesus. I stated emphatically who I am because of Christ and His Spirit within me and His anointing upon me. I spoke quietly so as not to attract any nurse's attention. But I spoke very strongly, firmly, and decisively with clarity of purpose and intention. I knew who I was "in Christ." I knew the power of God's Word that I spoke out. I made sure those thirty demons were aware of who I was and the power of God's Word that I was quoting!

How did I know there were thirty demons in the room? Physically, I could not see them. Demons are spirit beings; therefore, they are inanimate—no physical body. But in my spirit, I knew without doubt that there were thirty demons in the room.

My comments went something like this: "You demons know who I am, and I know who you are. I am a child of the living God. I carry the authority and power of Jesus, the Christ. Jesus whipped Satan in hell 2,000 years ago and took the keys of death and hell away from him. I carry the authority of Jesus and the power of His name and Word with me. In the name of Jesus, all of you, demons, get out of this room!" I was standing about one step inside the room. At that strong command, the demons began to leave. It seemed a physical feeling, but it may have been more of a spiritual sense. I could feel them go by me as they left the room. Swish, swish, swish. They were passing by me and out the door.

When the swishing stopped, I looked around the room. It was clear of demons. *Uh oh,* I thought, *there are three demons hiding behind that big medical equipment on the opposite side of the bed.* I walked around the bed, where I could see behind the medical equipment. Physically, I could see nothing, but I knew that those demons were now exposed. I spoke angrily to them, "I know that you are trying to hide from me, but I can see you now. In the name of Jesus, get out of this room and don't come back!" Those three demons left.

Looking carefully around the room, I sensed that the demons that had been in the room were gone. Next, I walked around the bed to where Nellie lay. After sixteen days and the demons cast out of the room, she was still unconscious. When I laid my hands on her bare arm, I realized, "She has demons in her!" I started talking strongly, commanding those demons to come out of her. They would not budge. The first twenty-two demons in the room consisted of the equivalent of privates, corporals, and sergeants. The demons in Nellie were the "officers," the leaders. They knew their authority and power, also. They would not let go and leave her.

The Christian's spiritual authority is embodied in God's Word. I had to strongly call on the "sword of the Spirit, God's written Word" (Ephesians 6:17, NASB). I began to quote more scripture commanding those demons to come out of her. After an estimated two to three minutes, three of the lower-ranking officer demons left Nellie. I spoke more of God's Word with authority, purpose, and intention. Two more demons released their grip and came out of Nellie. I knew in my spirit that there were more demons still in her. It took another estimated five minutes of spiritual warfare, quoting God's Word with strength and determination, to get control of these last three demon leaders. Finally, the last three demons left Nellie's body. In my spirit, Nellie now felt fresh and clean. The entire room was now fresh and clean, demon-free.

I began to preach to Nellie as if I had a full audience, filling her with God's written Word and the Holy Spirit. Again, I spoke quietly yet intently and firmly. I did not want to be distracted by nurses or anyone else coming into the room. The purpose for this is stated in Matthew 12:43–45. She was now clean of evil, demonic spirits, so I filled her with God's Word so the evil demon spirits could not come back to dwell in her again. After about a ten-to-fifteen-minute sermon, I anointed Nellie with oil representing the Holy Spirit, prayed for her, and left. All this time, Nellie was totally unconscious, showing no indication that she knew what was happening or even having heard a word that I had said. I was operating strictly in faith in the truth of God's Word.

The following day, I ministered to Nellie again. Nellie and her ICU room were still fresh and clean, free of demons. She was still unconscious, showing no indication that I had been in the room. I preached to her for about ten minutes, anointed her with oil, and left. On the third day, the same procedure, same apparent results. At least she was living far longer than what the doctor had expected. Each day, I would also minister to her mother, husband, and various relatives and friends who came to visit her.

On the fourth day, as I preached to Nellie, she slowly raised one eyelid about half open and then let it close. This was the first sign of physical life that she had shown. This excited me. I said, "Nellie, if you can hear me, open your eye again." Slowly, the eyelid opened. After following God's Word strictly in faith that Nellie, the spirit being, could hear me, now I saw the physical results. *Boom* went my faith. The truth and power of God's Word were obviously working. Each day after that, I would preach to Nellie, anoint her with oil, and pray for her. Each day, she showed more physical progress. She began to move her arms and then talk to me. Her strength was gradually returning. Doctors, nurses, and especially family were overjoyed with her recovery. So was I!

An amusing thing for me happened one day after Nellie was beginning to show physical signs of life. During the visit, she opened her eyes and listened as I preached to her, prayed for her, then turned to leave. Nellie slowly raised her right arm and touched her forehead. She wanted me to anoint her with oil. I was impressed and a bit amused. She had remembered the oil even though I had forgotten it.

As Nellie's strength increased to where we were holding conversations, one day, I questioned her concerning what may have happened in her life that would allow these demons to enter her, possess her, and bring her to the point of death. I was very curious about the cause. Some pastors teach that a Christian cannot become demon-possessed or controlled because of their acceptance and submission to Christ. They teach that, in effect, the Christian is "Holy Spirit-possessed or controlled." As a result, demons cannot possess a Christian.

Nellie told me that her favorite TV programs were soap operas. She watched soap opera programs all day, every day. She knew in detail about the various characters, both male and female. She knew the program plots and plot developments. She even subscribed to five different soap opera magazines and always read them. Nellie had become deeply involved with soap operas physically, mentally, emotionally, and even spiritually. She unknowingly had allowed demons into herself through the influence of soap operas.

This was about 1987. I had noticed when watching soap operas at a relative's house around 1970 that they were immoral in nature. At that time, I considered them to be the most immoral programs on television, at least that I was familiar with. Nellie had totally immersed herself in the "soap opera culture." It almost cost her life.

I told Nellie that if she wanted to live a normal, healthy life, then she must cancel the magazine subscriptions, burn all the magazines and never, ever watch another soap opera. This caused an emotional upset with Nellie. But she did finally agree to do what I had told her. I also told her to develop a daily Bible reading program to fill herself with the knowledge and character of God. This would strengthen her not only spiritually but also mentally, emotionally, and physically. Daily, I ministered to Nellie and occasional family members. Three months after first seeing Nellie unconscious and at the point of death, she walked out of the hospital healthy and strong. I have learned that "time" is an important factor to consider when ministering healing to someone.

God, through the truth and power of His Word and love, had saved her life. I thanked God for using me as His representative in those circumstances. I also thanked Him for all I had learned through following the precedents set by Jesus. As Jesus was daily led by the Holy Spirit, I recognized that I, too, had been daily led by the Holy Spirit. God is a God of love.

His Word is true. We each just need to learn His Word and how to use it.

Demons are more common in our lives than most people, including ministers, realize. In Phase 7 of this book, more experiences with demons in people are described.

What is the purpose of demons on earth and in people's lives? They are sent by Satan, the devil, to do his will. Satan's character and nature is "to steal, kill and destroy" (John 10:10, NASB). "Satan is a liar and the father of lies. There is no truth in him" (John 8:44, NASB).

Jesus came so "that we may have life and have it abundantly." Jesus, speaking to His original twelve disciples, said, "Truly, truly, I say to you, he who believes in Me, the works that I do shall he do also; and greater works than these shall he do; because I go to the Father" (John 14:12, NASB). Speaking to His disciples after His resurrection, Jesus said, "In My name they will cast out demons" (Mark 16:17, NASB). Christians are disciples of Jesus. I am a Christian. So, when the occasion demands, I cast out demons.

Drug Overdoses

It seemed that each time that I went to the hospital, something unexpected would happen. Often, it was the "unusual"! I never knew what to expect. At each thirty-two-mile round trip, I would pray in the Spirit for most of the sixteen miles going there. On the return drive home, I would praise God for His using me, teaching me, and healing people. Ephesians 6:18 (NASB) says, "Pray in the Spirit at all times." Jude 1:20 (NASB) states, "Building yourselves up on your faith; praying in the Holy Spirit." Praying in the Spirit is praying in tongues, as happened on the Day of Pentecost.

As I prayed, my faith would be "built up" or increased for that particular occasion. It was also being increased overall. With these experiences, God was not only building my faith but also teaching me how to work with people, specifically hospital patients, their friends and families, doctors and nurses. This training has proved valuable on many occasions through the years since then.

During one hospital visit, I was told about a young lady who had accidentally overdosed on drugs. I asked the Holy Spirit if I should seek family permission to pray for her. His reply was, "Why are you here?" Of course, I was at the hospital to pray for or minister to people in whatever capacity was needed. I went to the young lady's room. She lay in bed under an oxygen tent, totally unconscious. Tubes and IVs were in her arms and mouth. I introduced myself to her mother and father who were sitting in the room with very worried and stressful expressions on their faces. At my request to pray for the girl, they seemed to have the attitude of "Well, it can't hurt. Go ahead." They told me this: "The doctors have not given us any hope at all. It is not likely that she will recover. If she does come out of the coma, what kind of mental condition will she be in?"

I had already asked the Holy Spirit how to pray for the young lady, and He told me. With the parents seeming reluctant permission, I laid hands on her bare arm, anointed her with oil, and prayed as He had previously directed me. The Holy Spirit spoke to me and said, "She will recover and be mentally healthy." I told the parents, "Your daughter will recover and be mentally healthy." They looked at me as if I had no idea of what

I was saying. After all, they had heard the doctors' cautious comments. Politely, they thanked me. I told them, "I will be back tomorrow and pray for her again."

The next day, the young lady, though still under the oxygen tent, was conscious with her eyes open but could not talk because of the tubes. I spoke to her parents. They gave me the medical update. Then, I introduced myself to the girl. Next, I shared some of God's Word appropriate to her situation, then ministered healing and recovery to her. She seemed to accept what I had said and done.

On the third day, as I was driving to the hospital, I prayed for the girl, and God gave me a message for her. She had been transferred to a private room. This was an early evening visit rather than an afternoon, as were the previous two visits. Her parents were not there. The tubes had all been removed. She had showered and eaten meals. She also had applied a modest amount of facial makeup and combed her hair neatly. She felt good, was alert, and conversed quite well. She also remembered me from the previous day. In the presence of a male friend who was there visiting, I gave her this message. "While driving to the hospital, I was praying for you. God told me to tell you that you are a Christian, a child of His. You know better than to do drugs. It is harmful and a sin against your own self as well as a sin against God. God said that if you overdose on drugs again, He will *not* recover you. *You will die* because of what you have done to yourself." Her eyes were big, and her facial expression was one of overwhelming consternation and fear. She received fully the entire message. The boyfriend was visibly impressed also. I shared some scripture with her as directed by the Holy Spirit, then prayed for her. She thanked me and said that she was scheduled to be released from the hospital the next morning. She seemed very grateful for the ministry and health recovery that God had granted her. I never saw nor heard from the young lady again.

When God gave me the message to tell the young lady that she would die if she overdosed on drugs again, I thought, *This is a powerful message! What kind of reaction will she have to this? Will she receive what I tell her? Will she tell me that I am some kind of fool? Will there be total rejection? Or will there be acceptance?* How was I to know? I did know clearly what God had told me. Was I going to be obedient and deliver the message as spoken to me? Was I going to succumb to doubt and fear and not deliver the message? That would be disobedience. Long ago, I had committed to complete obedience to whatever God directed me to do. It would take courage, much courage! But I chose to be obedient. I chose to deliver that life-or-death message to the young lady. As a result of that obedience to God, confidence, courage, and a certain amount of boldness developed. I would need all of that to handle some unusual situations in future years.

In this testimonial, I have chosen to relate various events that had a particular, long-lasting impact on me. Then, I explained that impact, the effect that it had on me, and what I learned from each event as best as I could. There were so many events that happened during those Seven Phases of Training, which lasted a period of fourteen years, that as stated at the end of the Gospel of John, "If they were written in detail, I suppose that even the world itself would not contain the books which were written" (John 21:25, NASB). I realize this is an exaggeration, but sometimes, this is how I feel. When you don't know much, there is very, very much that needs to be learned. Just what does God have planned for me that I need to learn these lessons from the many, many experiences? Someday, I suspect that I will look back on time and experiences and think, *Oh! Now I understand.* It is all on God's time and for His purposes. It is His plan, not mine.

A Second Drug Overdose

On one of the hospital visits, I ministered to several people as had become common. Walking in a hallway, I passed a group of maybe five to six people, probably in their early twenties and early thirties. They were obviously in deep felt emotional upsets. I asked the Holy Spirit, "May I minister to these people?" No answer. A few minutes later, I was returning down the same hallway. I asked again, "Holy Spirit, is there something that You want me to tell these people?" Again, no answer. When going to various rooms to minister to several different individuals, I passed the group of people a third time. "Holy Spirit, isn't there something that I can share with these people? Obviously, they need support." Still, no answer. When I finished ministering in a room and was walking down the hall again, there they were, still standing, crying and talking. This fourth time, I questioned the Holy Spirit. Still, no answer.

I had completed all the ministering for that day and was headed toward the door and parking lot to go home. A fifth time, I see these people ahead of me in the hallway. A fifth time, I spoke to the Holy Spirit. "Holy Spirit, this is the fifth time that I have passed this group of people in the hallway. They are seriously upset about something. I am headed to the door and home. I won't see them again. Isn't there something

You would have me share with them? Please give me a scripture, a comment, or whatever You want." One scripture came into my spirit. This scripture came to me only faintly rather than the clear and definite way I was more familiar with. I stopped and introduced myself to the group. Then, I shared with them the scripture that the Holy Spirit had given me. They began to explain that a lady relative had deliberately overdosed on drugs of some kind to kill herself. The doctors, professionally cautious, were offering no hope of recovery. This group consisted of sons, daughters, nieces, and nephews. As I listened to them and repeated the one scripture, more came to me from the Holy Spirit. As the scriptures came into my spirit, I listened to their comments and answered their questions. After giving them "hope" based on God's Word, I prayed with and for them. Also, I declared a complete recovery for the patient.

The next day, some of the same group were in the same hallway area. They were eager to see me. Much conversation, including their comments, questions, and my scriptural answers, came forth. Their relative was recovering. Now, they had hope both in the natural and spiritual realms. They were excited and wanted to hear more of the "good news of Jesus." One comment from one of the young men was, "I have been to several churches and even read the Bible some. But I hardly understand any of it. It is very confusing. But Jerry, you make it really simple. You explain the Bible, so it is easy to understand." How encouraging to me. God was using me effectively, as stated in His original call for me to preach. "You shall go speak. You shall speak to one or two, four or five, one hundred or two hundred, a thousand or more." Doing this hospital ministry,

I was regularly speaking to one or two, four or five. This is not how the typical evangelist ministers. I was not speaking to crowds of people and getting many salvations as so often happens in evangelistic ministry. But I was ministering in the manner God had told me. It was obviously effective. Praise God!

On the third day, I again shared scripture, answered questions, and listened to their comments. Also, I prayed for them. Due to the particular circumstances of her case, I never did get to meet and minister directly to the lady patient. But she had been prayed for by me and her relatives. We were all in strong agreement for her recovery. The next day, I was informed that she had gone home fully recovered. Like so many others, I never heard from nor saw any of the group again.

Altogether, during the one-year hospital ministry, there was a total of five people who were on life support with no hope given by the doctors for recovery. Being guided by the Holy Spirit about what, when, and how to minister to those people, four walked out of the hospital fully recovered. As mentioned earlier, the fifth "life support patient, Ted, rolled out of the hospital in his wheelchair." He lived nine more years and died of "natural causes."

Does this mean that I now know how to minister to the desperately ill—and they will always recover? *No!* What it does mean is this: I learned to rely totally on the Holy Spirit. So often, I had no natural idea how to minister in the many and varied situations. So, I prayed, then took time to listen to God and was obedient to minister as He directed me. It all had to do with faith in and communication with God. I believe the principle in the statement by the apostle Paul, as recorded in 2 Corinthians 12:9–10 (NASB), was and is appropriate for me in those types of circumstances. "God has said to me,' My grace is sufficient for you, for power is perfected in weakness.' 'For when I am weak, then I am strong.'"

You probably have noticed that I constantly refer to the Holy Spirit. Does this mean that I am leaving Jesus out of my ministry experiences? Certainly not! Am I leaving God out or elevating the Holy Spirit above God? Most certainly not! God sent Jesus to earth more than 2,000 years ago. Jesus exhibited and expressed God's love, healing, and deliverance power during His thirty-three and a half years of life here on earth. This included His three and a half years of ministry. Jesus set the precedent for Christians of every generation. After all, Jesus did say, "You shall do the things that I have done and even greater things than these" (John 14:12, NASB).

Jesus also made the statement, as recorded in John 16:7 (NASB), "But, I tell you the truth, it is to your advantage that I go away; for if I do not go away, the Helper shall not come to you; but if I go, I will send Him to you!"

As we study the four Gospels and Hebrews, we find that after His death and resurrection, Jesus ascended back to heaven and is seated at the right hand of God, which is the position of honor. After His ascension, *Jesus sent the Holy Spirit to earth!* This is recorded in Acts 2:1–4. The Holy Spirit, God in Spirit form, is still here on earth! So yes, I refer to the Holy Spirit often and rely on Him. Without Him, I can do nothing! Jesus made the strong statement recorded in John 15:5 (NASB): "I am the vine. You are the branches. He who abides in Me and I in him, he bears much fruit; for apart from me, you can do nothing!" Jesus, the Holy Spirit, and God are One. Each has

His own function. The Holy Spirit is referred to in the Bible as the Spirit of God and also as the Spirit of Christ. When I refer to one of them, in reality, I am referring to all three, for the "three are one." But I do recognize that one function of the Holy Spirit is to enable the Christian to do the things that Jesus did. He enables us to carry out the supernatural commands of God. "[F]or apart from Me you can do nothing" (John 15:5, NASB). I find that carrying out the works of Jesus is very exciting. I praise God often for calling and appointing me to do His work.

Deliverance

One other supernatural and spectacular healing that God used me in during the one-year hospital ministry comes to mind. I believe it is worth relating. A couple we had met at Victory Christian Center in Tulsa asked me to go to Oral Roberts University Hospital and minister healing to their son. He was what is often described today as independent and rebellious, living his own life. He would have nothing to do with this "church stuff." The young man preferred to "party," which included heavy drinking, drugs, smoking, and "doing his own thing." Apparently, his mom and dad were having very little influence on their son's lifestyle now that he was a grown man. Still, they loved their son and were very concerned about him.

This young man had something seriously physically wrong with his body. The doctors had run tests of many kinds for five days yet were unable to determine the cause of his rapidly declining health. If this health decline continued, there was fear that he would die in only a few days. At his parent's request, I went to visit the young man in his hospital room on Friday, the evening of the fifth day of his hospital stay. I did a lot of praying and listening before the hospital visit but received nothing concerning what to do from the Holy Spirit. But, in faith of God and at the parents' request, I went. I felt totally helpless. Entering his room, I introduced myself and then sat down for a casual visit. After several minutes, and I had not "preached" to him, he seemed to relax, and we had a pleasant visit for about thirty minutes.

I gently questioned the young man concerning past Christian teaching or influence. With the unexpected freedom to express himself without criticism, he communicated his thoughts and views openly. Listening to his comments, I began to weave into our conversation the principles of salvation. I was careful not to use King James language, Bible chapters, verses, or "religious" terms. He was open and receptive to this approach. Soon, I prayed with him for his salvation. Also, I spoke healing, recovery of health, and deliverance from drugs, alcohol, and tobacco to him. Again, I was careful not to use "religious" terms that might create confusion or conflict. After a few more moments of pleasant conversation, I excused myself and left.

The next morning, the doctors could find nothing wrong with him physically and mentally. So, they released him, and he went home. When I would see the parents after that, they always expressed gratitude and were overjoyed that their son was healthy and had received his salvation. As with so many other people, I never saw the young man nor heard from him after that evening in the hospital.

In this salvation and deliverance experience, glory for the positive results must go to God. Other than what I have just expressed, I certainly cannot take any credit. If I were confronted with a similar situation, I would not know what to do. Pray, be sensitive to the Holy Spirit. Do what seems appropriate at the time. Praise God for His supernatural power in action today.

During the course of the years of hospital ministry, many more people were ministered to with supernatural healing and other results. These five, whose stories I have detailed, were the most spectacular to me. I was only doing what I understood God wanted me, a new minister, to do. Nine years later, God clearly, distinctly informed me that this hospital ministry was Phase Three of training for the ministry that He had planned for me.

I have always found it interesting that this hospital ministry started with a request or invitation. I went back each day at the request or invitation of the patient or their relatives. After this young man's salvation-deliverance just described, the invitations to minister at the hospital ended. I never attempted to get more hospital invitations to St. Francis or any other hospital.

Phase 4
Evangelism on the Job

While living in Broken Arrow, OK, and attending Rhema, one of the companies that I worked for was DTL Movers. A former Rhema student had established a furniture moving company. I worked as a loader and truck driver for several months. Then, I moved into a position as the company's first full-time salesman. During the summer months, residential moving is very active. Preparations for the school year to end, close to Memorial Day weekend, start the summer activity. Labor Day week and the beginning of fall school term ends the fast-paced summer moving activity. This coincides with the public schools being closed during June, July, and August.

My responsibility was to inventory the furniture and other possessions to be moved from a home, determine time and costs, and any other essential factors. With this completed, I would then sell our moving services to the customer. Once a sale was completed with the contract signed, if I deemed it appropriate, I would talk with the customer about whatever was practical from a Christian perspective. This was an unusual, unique type of evangelism. First and foremost, I was working for the benefit of the company. The second critical consideration was the customer I had sold our services to. Understanding that God is love and He is vitally concerned with every individual, I very carefully presented Him to every customer who seemed interested or that I could influence. I learned to be painstakingly diligent with these efforts.

Moving is a time of emotional turmoil. Families are going through the time, trouble, and expense of moving within their cities or states to another state or occasionally to a foreign country. A myriad of decisions must be made, expenses taken care of, new jobs sometimes with new companies considered, and children change schools. There are a great number of factors to be considered. The decisions to be made are critical and numerous. Moving is a time of emotional turmoil for the entire family. How could I help them achieve peace within these circumstances?

Jesus is described as "Prince of Peace" by the prophet Isaiah in the Old Testament. I assumed the responsibility of projecting the peace of Jesus, the Messiah, to customers. Every customer was not open to receiving scriptural counsel. I quickly learned to listen to the conversation, statements, and attitude of the customer. Often, it could quickly be determined if the person or couple was open to receiving counsel.

First and foremost, I was a salesman representing my employer. Also, I was paid by commission. It meant money in my pocket not to miss a sale. Selling the company's services was what I did to earn wages for myself and income for the company. Satisfying the customer was essential to success. As I went about the task of property inventory and the other sales details, I listened to the customers' conversations. What was important to them? Many people reject anyone attempting to share Christian values because of not wanting to mix "religion" with business, denominational differences, or many and varied other reasons. I soon learned to integrate Christian principles into conversation without sounding "religious." The uniqueness of the type of evangelism that God had called me into was taking effect. I was daily speaking to one or two, four or five.

Soon, I was learning when and how to effectively share Jesus and His peace with customers at the end of a sales call. I also learned when to keep my mouth shut. Not everybody wants to hear the good news of Jesus, no matter how much turmoil and emotional upset their moving circumstances cause. Remember, I was getting paid to sell the company's moving services, not preach to the customer.

Since God spoke to me and said, "You shall go speak…" I have had a burning desire to do that. No matter where I am, who I am with, or what we are doing, out of me comes God's Word. Some people are so fervent about their business, career, family, or hobbies that they cannot refrain from talking about them. With me, it is the "call" to minister that God has given me. Sometimes, I tell people, "Be careful. If you bump into me, out will come God's Word." I do not do the work of the ministry in order to become a minister. I know who I am and what my life is about. "Out of who I am, I go and do." Within this understanding of who I am, I have learned a certain amount of discipline concerning when to speak out for God and when not to speak out. "On the job" is not always the best time to speak out for God. But I do contend that every Christian should be alert to that opportunity.

One of the principles emphasized to the student body during the first week's instruction at Rhema was the four points of order:

1. God must be first and foremost in your life.
2. Family, wife, then children must be second.
3. Job is third.
4. Ministry must be number four in order of importance.

These stated points of order created confusion, disagreement, and conflict among some of the students, particularly when first stated to the student body. Many students were adamant that ministry should be second in order, then family and job. In brief, the teaching was:

1. If you have been called into the ministry, then God must be first and foremost in your entire life.
2. Wife and family must be second in order of life importance. Due to disorder and conflict in the family, the ministry will suffer and possibly fail. So, maintain your family.
3. If the ministry income is not sufficient to provide full living expenses, a minister must work, hold a job, part-time or full-time, in order to provide sufficient living expenses for his family.
4. With your relationship with God taken care of, your wife and children loved, fed, and clothed, and a home provided for them, now you can afford to minister.

I worked part-time for several days with a man who disagreed with these priorities. He was adamant that the ministry must be second in order. In a brief time, this man had been fired from three jobs because of spending so much time "ministering to other workers." I explained to him that the company was not paying him to minister to people. He was getting paid to "load trucks." Before long, he was fired from that job, also. He would not accept the Rhema instruction that "A company pays you to do a job, not preach on the job. Do a good job. Make your employers' money. Work on company time. Witness and minister on your time." If every employee witnesses or ministers to other employees rather than working, production dwindles, and the company will eventually go broke. Then, the employees lose their jobs. This man definitely had God's call for the ministry on his life and was knowledgeable of the Bible. To me, he was interesting to talk to. I always enjoy hearing somebody share God's Word. But not everybody is as enthusiastic to hear as me, especially the non-Christians. Many people at work were more enthused with their jobs than hearing Christian principles. When you are zealous for the Lord, it sometimes requires strong self-discipline to not spend time ministering on the job. But it must be done. The lesson must be learned.

Many opportunities to minister in some capacity arose that I could take appropriate advantage of. People were ministered to for peace, salvation, physical healing, financial stability, job stability, baptism of the Holy Spirit, and numerous other desires and needs.

On one customer call, I noticed that the lady had something on her mind besides the business of the move. Perceiving that she had something important on her mind, I encouraged the lady to express herself. She began to give me her testimony of a miraculous recovery from death. By her mother and young adult son's account, this lady had died and been dead for an estimated ten minutes, then recovered before their very eyes. "I had been an invalid confined to a wheelchair for three years. Crippling arthritis had gradually become so severe that I had to be helped in and out of bed. A caregiver would have to assist me in and out of the bathroom, dress me, and even feed me. If a soup spoon was handed to me, with maximum effort, I could bend over and manage to get a spoonful of soup to my mouth. I could not use a knife and fork. My food had to be cut in bite sizes and fed to me."

"One day, my mother was caring for me. My grown son, stationed in the army at Ft. Sill, Lawton, Oklahoma, was 'home on leave.' I told them both that I felt tired and wanted to take a nap. I asked them to put me in bed and hand me my Bible, which was on the nightstand next to my bed. It was my habit to read a few scriptures before going to sleep. While reading, I quickly dozed off to sleep. I did not know that I had gone to sleep. I definitely was not aware that I had quit breathing and my heart had stopped beating, as later described by my mother and son. I just knew that I was passing through a large, long tunnel. As I emerged from the tunnel, a voice of 'love and power' spoke to me from within an extremely bright, white, yet soft light. The voice said, 'I give you back your life and health.' I woke up and, noticing my mother and son crying, asked, 'Why are you crying?' Surprised, astonished, and amazed, they replied, 'About ten minutes ago, you quit breathing, and your heart stopped beating. How can you be alive and talking to us now? You were dead!' I said, 'Well, I am not dead now. I am hungry. I am going to the kitchen and fix myself something to eat.' I threw back the bed covers and started to get out of bed. They quickly and excitedly exclaimed, 'You cannot get out of bed; you will fall!' They hurried to my bedside and tried to stop me from getting up. I said, 'Hand me my robe. I am going to the kitchen.' They helped me get dressed, and we went to the kitchen, where I fixed myself a sandwich and then ate it by myself. That was about three years ago. Since then, I have been able to do almost anything that I want to. I choose not to do anything heavy, like moving furniture. That is why I called your company. I just want to rearrange the furniture in several rooms, and I need somebody to do the heavy work. My husband is Catholic, and I am a Protestant. Due to his insistence, we attend the Catholic church. The priest graciously arranged to have some men carry me in my wheelchair up and down the many steps each Sunday morning. The priest always shook hands with the parishioners as we left services each Sunday. The Sunday after my miraculous healing, I walked up the church steps without aid. The priest was at the door. I took the time to give him my testimony. His response was, 'I have seen the physical condition that you have been in during the past few years. But I cannot believe the testimony that you just gave me.'"

Before leaving her house, I prayed with the lady to receive the baptism of the Holy Spirit. She started praying in tongues right then. By the time I returned to the company office, this lady had called, stating that I had left my business notebook at her house. My employer commented excitedly, "I don't know what happened at that lady's house, but when she called about your notebook, she was on such a 'spiritual high' that it even inspired me. Tell me what happened!"

Working in a Christian environment was a new and pleasant experience. The spiritual atmosphere was entirely different than what I was used to. People were more positive, had definite goals in mind, and were usually more diligent about doing a good job. I enjoyed working among Christians. After all, my entire life had changed. Now, I had a clear and definite relationship with God, rather than just knowing about Him. As I read the Bible, the people spoken of became real-life characters. I could identify with them instead of just reading about those people. I often thought, *How vastly different it is to work in this Christian environment.* There were many unusual and unique opportunities to minister to people while on this sales job. I was rapidly learning when to speak out for God and when not to.

In the past, I had taught in the public school system for twelve years. Although there were many worthwhile experiences and sound relationships developed during those twelve years, it was much different than working among all "Spirit-filled Christians." Some of the school personnel were Christians. A few were what I now define as committed Christians. Many of them were people who only worked hard at doing a good job and getting along with the other school personnel. They were people with a clear sense of right and wrong who were living and working in harmony with their fellow workers. But so often, they were not Christians who conscientiously applied Christian principles to the various aspects of life or work. For instance, I don't ever remember a group of teachers coming together and praying each day before school started.

I don't recall teachers involved in a particularly stressful situation praying together to seek God's direction about how to handle the problem. At DTL Movers, this was a common daily occurrence. We made sure that we were in agreement with each other and with God when we started the day. In addition, before one of the crews left to perform a residential or commercial move, they gathered in a group and prayed. The prayers were always specific for the job at hand and the customers to be served.

During those days in the public school system, I, too, was not a "committed Christian." At eight years old, I had accepted Jesus as my Lord and Savior. I was secure in my belief that if any tragedy causing premature death happened in my life, I would go to heaven. However, I was not committed and knowledgeable to the point that I was instrumental in guiding other people into salvation or regularly being a Christian influence on them. Isaiah 61:10 refers to garments of salvation and robes of righteousness. "I will rejoice greatly in the Lord, my soul will exalt in my God; for He has clothed me with garments of salvation, He has wrapped me with a robe of righteousness, as a bridegroom decks himself with a garland, and as a bride adorns herself with her jewels" (Isaiah 61:10, NASB). To develop righteousness took a stronger commitment and far deeper knowledge of God's character and nature than I was aware of. I am not sure that at that time in my life, I could even give a definition of biblical righteousness. Now, I define the term as "being acceptable to God" or "in right standing with God." At that time in my life, I did not know the Bible well enough to know what was righteous and what was unrighteous.

Thinking back, I liked to think at that time, I had an open mind. Now, I would say that I believed and lived the following: "Right-Wrong Principle." Everybody, including me, believes they are right in what they believe and what they do—how they live their lives. Nobody wants to be *wrong*. If I or anybody else thought they were wrong, then we would change. With the change in believing or doing, now we are *right*. So—I am always right—ha ha.

Working with and listening to the employees at DTL Movers, there were constant adjustments taking place in my beliefs, attitudes and the daily application of those beliefs and attitudes. Was I *right*—or *wrong?* Did I need to adjust again or completely change? Today, in this particular situation, am I right or wrong? Do I have the open mind that I like to think I have? Am I living my life in love so that joy and peace are constant within me? If not, why not? Do I project love and harmony or discontent and conflict? The employer and employees were being a constant, overall, positive influence on me. Obviously, I needed to learn and change in some areas of my life. Little did I know how God was using my time and experience at Dedicated to the Lord Movers. He was developing and maturing me. Transformation of my soul was taking place. Romans 12:2 (NASB) states, "You be transformed by the renewing of your mind." The mind, will, and emotions are identified as the "soul of man." My habits, attitudes, and emotions were each changing, being tempered, through my experiences working at DTL.

With all that I was learning through the four years of varied experiences while attending Rhema, I thought that I was ready for full-time ministry. I had no concept of how much more needed to be learned. One of the things that I learned was that I was not the only person capable of witnessing effectively. God was speaking to other people about ministry effectiveness, also. Although I was always wanting to share the "good news of Jesus," I soon learned that I did not have to do it all. As I watched the employees at DTL Movers share, witness, and minister so effectively, some of the "hot air" was being released from my ego. God was using other people, both men and women, at least as effectively as He was using me. The arrogance, the thoughts of how important I am because of how God was maturing me, was gradually being removed from me. It is important to "know who you are in Christ." It is important to know what you can do while working with the truth and power of God's Word. I call it "quiet confidence or self-assurance." It is at least as important as not getting into false pride. The book of Proverbs speaks strongly against false pride. "Pride goes before destruction and a haughty spirit before stumbling" (Proverbs 16:18, NASB). The book of James 4:6 (NASB) states, "God is opposed to the proud, but gives grace to the humble." James 4:10 (NASB) clarifies this principle even more: "Humble yourselves in the presence of the Lord and He will exalt you."

How do you operate as a minister with the strength and power that Jesus operated with and not get into false pride? The Amplified Bible helped clarify this question for me. Philippians 4:13 (AMP) states, "I have strength for all things in Christ who empowers me [I am ready for anything and equal to anything through Him who infuses inner strength into me; I am self-sufficient in Christ's sufficiency]." As I studied Jesus as a leader, how humble He was, yet how strong He was,

I realized that even as humility developed in me, I could be strong. Humility comes from strength within. These characteristics were being developed in me as I worked with the people at DTL Movers and continued to learn how to effectively minister to their customers.

Phase 5

Truck Driving Cross Country

With the summer moving season over, business slowed to where my income at DTL Movers dropped from 15 to 20 percent of what it was during the summer months. For financial reasons, I had to do something different. I had to find another job that would pay well. My family still wanted to eat regularly. Teenage appetites increase as teenagers grow. I quit the sales job. Often, employers are more likely to hire a person with a job who wants to change jobs rather than hire a person who is out of work. At the time, my thinking was, *I need full free time to find a good-paying job.*

Linda and I are strong on the value of husband-wife communication. I had not expressed my desire to Linda to quit this job to be free to seek a different job. Quitting the sales job without discussing the decision with Linda caused an emotional upset with her. It seemed to Linda that a little income from the sales job was better than no income if I quit the job. With family finances being tight, her attending Bible school, and our other struggles, it was unwise to do anything that might cause emotional conflict with the other spouse. But I had done just that. *Whoops!* I needed to do something quickly that would give her peace and calm and soothe her disturbed emotions. I needed to find a good-paying job!

After what seemed like a long time of finances getting worse and a lot of prayer, I talked to Kermit Hoffmeier, owner of a growing trucking company in Tulsa. Previously, I had driven a truck for a friend who had the truck leased to Hoffmeier Trucking Company. Mr. Hoffmeier put me to work driving one of his trucks.

Our job was to haul various kinds of processed oil from the Sunoco Refinery in west Tulsa to various destinations in all states east of Oklahoma and a few states west of Oklahoma. We would haul 6,000 to 6,500-gallon loads in 18-wheel tanker trucks. Typically, a driver would load Monday morning at the refinery located in west Tulsa and be gone from home all week delivering loads. He would return to Tulsa on Friday evening and be off work for the weekend.

I remember praying during my first trip as I drove east on I-44: "God, I thank You for the job and the income it will provide. But God, You called me into the ministry. I want to minister full-time. I want to preach somewhere every Sunday morning, Sunday evening, and Wednesday night. I want to preach revivals and home Bible studies. As I do that, I am confident that You will provide my finances through the offerings at the church services. I am grateful for the income this job will provide, but God, this does not look like the ministry to me. Please find me some place to preach. I will be gone from home all week. Isn't there some church, some individuals on my trip this week who I can minister to? My wife and teenage kids are at home all week without me. I need to be there so I can be the influence on them that a husband and father needs to be. I know that the economy is weak all over Oklahoma. God, this is the only job that I could find in Tulsa. Again, I am grateful for the income that it will provide, but I want to minister in some capacity. Please find me someone to minister to or some place to minister while I am gone this week."

After praying in English and expressing everything that was on my mind that day, I would pray in the spirit (tongues) for miles and miles. At times, I had no idea how long I had been praying nor how far along the interstate highway I had driven. I had been in the spirit realm. As I checked the highway signs and mileage markers, my location was determined. During those prayer times, I never missed a turn nor "got lost" on the unfamiliar highways and states.

When you receive Jesus as your Lord and Savior, then the Holy Spirit comes to dwell (live or inhabit) within your physical body (1 Corinthians 3:16 and 6:19). Wherever you are, He is. When you have been baptized in the Holy Spirit, His anointing is upon you. Again, wherever you are, He is, with His anointing to enable you to do the things that Jesus did. Every day, as I drove along the highways, I prayed in the Spirit, building up my most holy faith (Jude 20). Wherever I stopped, I was already spiritually sensitive. It became a common occurrence as I sat in a truck-stop café eating a meal; I would look around the booths and tables, carefully observing the drivers, waitresses, people bussing tables, or whoever was in the room. My standard question was, "Holy Spirit, is there someone in the room who you want me to minister to?" As I observed the people, invariably, one individual would stand out, somehow different than everybody else. My next question was, "Holy Spirit, what do You want me to tell that person?" The Holy Spirit would give me a scripture, a word of knowledge, or a prophetic word of some kind. Then, I would pick up my coffee cup, go to the person, and deliver the message. This took courage, especially at first. When I was sure the Holy Spirit had spoken to me, it was a matter of "Am I going to be obedient or disobedient?" Remember, He is God in spirit form. God was not giving me these messages in a trivial manner. He intended for the message to be delivered. Someone needed to be ministered to, and I was the messenger. Was I going to overcome the fears, doubts, and apprehensions and deliver the message or not? After all, traveling along the highway, I had prayed and asked God to give me someone to minister to. I had asked the Holy Spirit to show me someone to minister to, then asked for the message. He gave me the message. Was I going to be obedient and deliver the message, or not?

Some of those drivers or other people were gruff and rugged in manner and appearance. I did not want to create a conflict of any kind. Often, especially the first few times this happened, it took a lot of courage. But the results were very rewarding. Sometimes, I would get this type of reaction, "Who told you that about me?" Or "How did you know that about me?" Some brief, but interesting conversations often would develop.

Although I was not aware of it at the time, God had me in a unique and specialized type of evangelistic training from the seat of the truck. Looking back, I have sometimes wondered, *Did these unusual ministry experiences happen as I remember?* I know without question that they did. Was I creating situations of my own initiative? They were so unusual. Was God actually directing me? When considering these questions, I remembered the story of Philip, the Evangelist, and the Ethiopian treasurer as related in Acts 8:26–40. Philip was directed by an angel. Angels are messengers sent by God. Philip was obedient to do what God's messenger, the angel, had told him. The result was a man was ministered to and received his salvation. God's purpose was fulfilled.

As I heard from God and was obedient and diligent to do what He commanded, God's purpose in each situation was fulfilled. I stayed alert to the opportunity to share the good news of Jesus wherever these trips on the truck took me. Dependent upon the particular type of oil to be loaded, gasoline, hydraulic fluid, motor oil, anti-freeze, etc., occasionally the tank would have to be steam cleaned. After getting this done one day, I pulled into a large oil refinery at Lake Charles, Louisiana. After showing the cleaning receipt to the two-man loading crew, they gave the tank a visual inspection and then a sniff test. Smelling nothing, they loaded the tank with the requested type of oil. After loading, a sample of the oil was taken from the full tank and sent to the company laboratory for verification of its purity. The lab test took approximately thirty minutes. It was time for their work shift to end, but the loaders had to wait until the lab tests were received. The three of us went to the "loaders shack" to wait for the test results. With nothing else to do, we casually "shot the breeze," questioning each other and commenting about our family lives. When I mentioned that I was an evangelist and had recently completed Bible school, my comments brought up many questions and comments from the two loaders.

The Word of God began to flow out of me. After a few minutes, one of the loaders withdrew from the conversation. In the small twelve by twelve feet room, he still heard all the conversation of the other loader and me. The interested loader and I carried on a conversation of questions, scriptural answers, and comments until the test results were received and they could leave. The uninterested man went his way. The interested loader asked for a ride through the refinery and out the gate to the parking lot where his car was parked.

As I carefully drove through the refinery, the loader began to talk. "I am a Christian, too. I belong to a church of about one hundred people and attend fairly regularly. In this refinery, there are about 3,500 employees. It seems like every one of them is foul-mouthed and negative-minded. I used to share my Christian beliefs, but the criticism and harassment became so regular and severe that, finally, I quit speaking out. It seemed as if everybody, all 3,500 of these men, were against me. Then, here you come in, a truck driver in work clothes, and begin to just casually, nonchalantly share the Scriptures and how it is a part of your daily life. You have been such an encouragement to me. I am going to start studying the Bible again and speaking out for God."

I both encouraged and cautioned him to use the principles in the Scriptures, not the King James language. "Truth is always effective and will change people's thinking and lives. The non-Christian, whether interested in biblical truths or not, will often reject those truths when it is presented in King James language, or you quote chapter and verse. From these people come the typical negative replies. 'Don't try to push your religion on me. You cannot prove to me there is a God. If there is a God in control of this world, why are there so many murders, robberies, rapes, etc.?' There is power and truth in God's Word. Learn His Word and speak the principles of His Word with the power of the Holy Spirit. That is what Jesus did. Look at the results He had. Remember, many people received what Jesus had to say. Many other people rejected what Jesus had to say. You won't be any different. Jesus spoke and lived God's truth in spite of criticism and rejection. Let me encourage you to do the same." I prayed for the man, and we parted.

I have often wondered how much spiritual strength was imparted to that man and what changes developed in him. Concerning the other loader who withdrew from the conversation, I have the same questions about him. As with Jesus, one person received, and one seemingly rejected. I had spoken to one and two. Without realizing the extent, I was fulfilling God's call on my life.

My natural mind kept thinking that I should be preaching to a church full of people. Yet, God had told me to speak to "one or two, four or five, one hundred or two hundred, a thousand or more." Looking back on time and experiences, some of my most effective ministering has been to the one or two, four or five. Also, I feel just as fulfilled ministering to the one or two, four or five, as when ministering to large crowds. At the time, this was all happening as I earned a living driving a truck cross country for Mr. Hoffmeier. Eventually, I would realize that as I stayed faithful, God was training me in Phase 5 of the ministry.

On another oil delivery trip, I stopped to eat at a big truck stop in Beaumont, Texas. I was scheduled to load at a local refinery the next morning, so I had plenty of time. I browsed the gift shop, then went into the café to eat the evening meal. As I sat eating, I looked around, asking the Holy Spirit who to minister to. No reply. By the time my meal was eaten, I was disappointed that the Holy Spirit had not spoken to me. At nearly every stop, He would give me a message for someone. It had become exhilarating. I expected Him to point out someone for me to minister to. Disappointed, I picked up my meal ticket and went to the cash register to pay. As I waited my turn, I noticed there was something special about the cashier, but I was not clear as to what it was. I paid the ticket and moved to the opposite wall in an attempt to be as inconspicuous as possible. There, I stood quietly "praying in the spirit" to become more sensitive to the Holy Spirit. After a few minutes, He began to speak to me about the cashier. When the customers had paid and she had free time, I walked to her workstation and introduced myself. I could read her thoughts. *Uh oh, here is a truck driver wanting personal time with me after work.* As I began to tell her what the Holy Spirit had told me about her character and personal situation, she relaxed and listened, quite surprised. I explained that I understood her initial reluctance to listen. She was neatly dressed and attractive, so she likely had to occasionally ward off would-be suitors.

I quickly stated my purpose for wanting a few minutes of her undivided attention. As I identified her positive and commendable character qualities, her spirit opened to all that I had to say. The Holy Spirit had given me a Word of Knowledge for the lady. This is one of the nine gifts of the Holy Spirit, as listed in 1 Corinthians 12:1–11. The message ended with some encouraging comments about the possibilities of her future.

This cashier was thrilled that God was interested enough in her that He would send some total stranger to tell her these things. To hear the description of how commendable these character qualities were was thrilling, inspirational, encouraging, and a life-changing blessing to the lady. As she had time between customers paying their tickets, the lady briefly described her former abusive marriage. She had secretly saved portions of grocery and other household money until she had enough to pay bus fare and estimated living expenses until she hopefully found a job that would pay her income sufficient to provide living expenses. She had packed one suitcase with essential personal items and secretly left her Chicago home. Her abusive husband would discover her gone when he arrived home from work that evening.

The lady explained how desperate she was to escape that unhappy marriage. She also briefly described how her life had changed for the better since she was alone and free from her past marriage. For a total stranger to relate the God-given message that I had related to her inspired her with a new and strong confidence. The lady was thrilled because of the message. I was thrilled because the Holy Spirit had used me to be an impact on someone's life.

I left the truck stop, drove for about thirty minutes, and located the loading area for the next morning. I found a safe and secure place to park the 18-wheel tanker truck, then crawled into the sleeper cab for a good night's rest. The sun would wake me the next morning in ample time to meet my loading schedule. As I lay in bed, I thanked God for using me.

What I learned in that situation was to be patient and stay in faith. The Holy Spirit does not always tell me everything, all the details, about a coming ministry situation in order to soothe my impatience. He operates when, where, and how He chooses. I must remain faithful and obedient.

Family at home—me hundreds of miles away each week.

I love my family and enjoy spending time with them. I enjoy being a husband and father. At whatever age each of the children has been, I have always enjoyed their companionship. I receive pleasure guiding and directing them as they each develop through life. Wanda, our oldest at twenty-six years old, is living in Albuquerque, New Mexico, about seven hundred miles distant. I had a standing request with the company dispatcher to haul any load scheduled for New Mexico. This would allow me to have an occasional visit with Wanda. Cheryl is eighteen and a freshman at Oral Roberts University, Tulsa, Oklahoma, only an hour's drive away from home. Paul is sixteen, a junior in high school, and plays football at the local high school. Janice will soon be fifteen. She is a freshman at the local high school and developing into leadership in her church teen group.

Paul and Janice "pick on each other." Janice will tease him, and Paul then will play "professional wrestler" with his pretty, petite younger sister. He picks her up, holds her over his head, then throws her on the couch. All this time, Janice is yelling, "Daddy, Daddy, make him stop!" Then she picks on him again, and the wrestling continues.

On the road away from home each week, I miss my family. I need and want to be home with them. But this cross-country truck driving job is all I could find that would pay a salary that would meet our needs. Linda had graduated from Rhema Bible Training School and took a public school teaching position thirty-two miles away from our new home in Chelsea, OK. Her salary, combined with mine, was bringing financial relief to our family. When I arrived home each weekend, she would immediately approach me with plans and problems of hers and the two teenage kids still living at home. This may have relieved stress from her, but it caused stress for me. After being gone all week, I wanted the pleasure of spending time with my family.

Linda and I discussed the situation. We developed this plan. When I arrived home, we would visit with each other, attend football games, attend church Sunday, and in general, refresh family relationships. During the previous week, as questions and activities arose, Linda would make decisions that were immediately necessary. She would also make a list of various activities and responsibilities that needed my input. We discussed this with Janice and Paul. We made one hard and firm rule that could not be broken. We, as a family, would have Sunday dinner in our home. The kids could invite any of their friends for dinner that they chose. We would eat a tasty meal and have a family visit. All questions and activities of the past week and the coming week would be discussed. Decisions would be made that were beneficial to the entire family. This turned out to be very beneficial and enjoyable for all of us. Sunday dinner time often included one to four school friends and occasionally Cheryl and a friend from college. One high school friend commented, "I like this family get-together. My family never gets together for a meal, discusses issues, laughs, and jokes like this. This is fun." This plan worked out very well for the entire family during the two years driving trucks cross country.

I was sent to southwest Texas with a load. On the way, I stopped to eat supper at a roadside café in the small town of Holly, a few miles west of Wichita Falls, Texas. The people in the small "down home" café were enjoyable to visit with as I ordered and ate my meal. Somehow, out came God's Word in the conversation. One man seemed particularly interested, so I invited him to bring his coffee and pie to my booth. This man questioned me about several subjects. His particular interest was "Does God want Christians to be prosperous? Is God punishing me for wrongdoing? What does the Bible say about divorce?" As his questions became more of a private and personal nature for him, he suggested that we go to his church, which was unlocked. We drove the two blocks in the man's car. As I gave the man scriptural answers to his questions, he became greatly relieved.

Due to competition and especially the local economy, this man's contracting business had begun to fail. When the business was close to total financial failure, his wife divorced him. So, his questions were quite serious. According to him, his life had become a failure. Was God punishing him by causing his business failure? Apparently, this man had received some very unsound and erroneous counsel. His entire attitude began to change as I gave him scripture and brief teachings on prosperity, divorce, and the character and nature of God.

The teaching went something like this. God is love. Out of His love, He wants each of us to be prosperous and healthy. But we must learn and use principles from the Bible. We must learn and use sound business practices. We must make sound business decisions. Timing concerning those decisions is critically important. Scriptural support for my remarks was 1 John 4:7–8, Deuteronomy 8:18, and 3 John 2.

"God's original plan was for one man to have only one wife for his lifetime. God hates divorce. Divorce is considered a sin. However, divorce is not an unforgivable sin. The only unforgivable sin is blasphemy against the Holy Spirit. Since you have been involved in a divorce, repent of that sin. Ask God to forgive you. God is quick to forgive, and He does not remember your sins. Forgive yourself. Go on with your life." Supporting scriptures were Genesis 3:24, Malachi 2:16, Luke 12:10, Isaiah 43:25, and Psalm 86:5.

During our conversation, I pointed out that when God punished His people, it was always after sin became worse and worse for several generations. God would always send His prophets to warn His people. When they refused to heed His warnings, then finally, God would punish His people. "Mr., I suggest that you do not qualify for God to get angry with you to the extent that He would punish you! Live your life in love and peace. Pray. Worship God. He wants to hear from you. God loves you."

I was excited about the opportunity to counsel the gentleman with God's Word. Like several other times since I went to work for Hoffmeier Trucking Co., I was traveling the highway in the 18-wheel truck, doing my job and praying as I drove. God created the opportunity for me to minister to the "one." Praise God. He was answering my prayers.

On one of these trips to locations in southwest Texas, I had delivered my load and was traveling east on I-10. Suddenly, I realized it was Wednesday, church night. Glancing at my watch, I saw the time was 6:45 pm. The typical mid-week church service time is 7:00 p.m. At the next exit, where a town of 3,000 to 4,000 population was located, I took the exit and began to look for any church with cars around it. I soon found a Baptist church. Within walking distance of the church was a gravel parking area big enough for the truck. God had answered my prayers.

I entered the church building just as the pastor opened the service. He was showing a video teaching on the "gifts of the Holy Spirit," as stated in 1 Corinthians 12:1–11. The video teacher was Reverend Adrian Rogers, then current president of the Southern Baptist Association. When attending Rhema Bible Training Center, founded by Kenneth E. Hagin, this was one of my favorite subjects. Kenneth Hagin and other Rhema instructors strongly emphasized the gifts of the Holy Spirit and God's supernatural power operating in the Christian's life. Reverend Adrian Rogers opened the teaching with Acts 1:8, a scripture referring to spiritual power. I thought, *This Baptist preacher must be knowledgeable of this subject.* I settled back in my seat, eager to hear the Baptist view of the gifts of the Holy Spirit.

All of my teaching was from the Pentecostal perspective. I was anxious to hear the Baptist perspective taught by the national president of the Southern Baptists. After a few comments concerning Acts 1:8, Reverend Rogers moved to Acts 2:1–4, the Day of Pentecost. This was another foundational scripture for the subject. My enthusiasm was increasing. After some standard comments concerning the Day of Pentecost, Reverend Rogers, in my opinion, went into a "speculative wonderland." He had no idea what he was talking about. He commented that running fast and jumping high were spiritual gifts. He made several other references to the "many, many spiritual gifts that God had given to man."

I thought, *Oh no. He is confusing spiritual gifts with physical abilities. Doesn't he know that spiritual matters are not physical in nature and cannot be described or explained in physical terms? Apparently not! Mercy me. These poor people don't know any different and are believing everything this man is teaching.* With my totally different Bible school background, I was flabbergasted. What could I do? What could I say to correct this terribly erroneous teaching?

After the video teaching was complete, the pastor made a few comments and then opened the floor to questions and comments. This was my chance. After a couple of the people made mild comments, I asked if I could comment. The pastor graciously gave me permission. I said, "I am an evangelist and a truck driver passing by your community. I am very pleased to hear Mr. Rogers teach on the gifts of the Holy Spirit. In 1 Corinthians 12:1–11, there are only nine Holy Spirit gifts listed in the Bible." My plan was to speak only two to three minutes expressing my appreciation for them allowing this total stranger to attend their service. But here I was getting wound up to preach "the truth" of the gifts of the Holy Spirit. My mouth began to get very dry to the degree that I realized that I must bring my comments to a close within one minute, or I would not be able to talk at all. I quickly completed my comments by thanking the pastor for letting this stranger speak. By the time my comments were concluded, my mouth and throat were so dry that I could not have uttered another sentence. I walked the few steps to my seat and sat down. My mouth and throat now had plenty of moisture. *What is going on with me?*

After the closing prayer and a few moments of friendly conversation, I walked to the truck, puzzled by the occurrence. As I drove along the interstate highway, I asked the Holy Spirit why my mouth became so dry that I could not talk. He made it very clear to me: "You were a guest and a stranger in that church. It was not your place to correct them and their teaching. You were getting very enthused as you spoke and would not stop when I nudged you. I had to shut you down."

The "right-wrong" principle that I mentioned earlier was strongly in action. They were biblically "wrong" in their teaching, and I was biblically "right." Right or wrong, it was not my place to correct them as I passed through their city and church. The Holy Spirit can handle that. He wants me to help, not hinder. As I reviewed all that had happened, I was reminded of the class at Rhema titled "Submission and Authority" taught by Keith Moore. That night, I was wanting to take authority because I was "right!" But it was not my place. There, in that situation, I needed to submit to the local church authority, who was the pastor. This was another lesson I learned as I drove the truck from location to location. When will I know enough, however much enough is?

The cross-country truck driving experiences ran from 1988 to 1990, covering close to two years. In those days, the best communication available among truck drivers was the Citizens Band Radio. A good quality radio had a communication range of two to three miles. As technology advanced, truck telephones came into use. In 2005, I worked for a few weeks on a pipeline construction job. By then, cell phones were in vogue.

All of the drivers from 1988 to 1990 had CB radios. It seemed critical or at least popular for every CB owner to have a "handle" (CB nickname) "so people could get a hold of you." Drivers were creative in selecting a "handle." After some thought, I decided my handle would be "Miracle Man." I developed a spiel that went something like this. A driver would ask, "What is your handle?" My reply was, "Miracle Man, my boss expects me to perform miracles."

"Yeah, that boss of mine expects me to perform miracles too. He thinks I can run 24/7 and still keep my logbook legal."

"My situation is probably a little different than yours. I drive this truck for Hoffmeier and Son with their headquarters in Tulsa, Oklahoma. But my primary job is preaching for Jehovah and Son with headquarters in the throne room in heaven." This verbal routine either brought about some interesting conversation or quickly stopped the conversation. But if I was on a job very long, everybody there knew about the Miracle Man.

The handle occasionally opened opportunities to minister one-on-one. Some people thought I was being arrogant or comical, or they had other reactions. But I knew the purpose of the "Miracle Man" handle! Regularly, God was performing miracles of some kind when I ministered in various ways. Another book will detail some of those miracles. We serve a miracle-working God.

Drive and pray. Drive and pray. After driving several hours, for me driving gets boring. Like other people, I sightsee as I travel. Having been along the interstate highways that I normally travel, monotony begins to take over. So, I pray. Prayer should be communication with God. So, I talk and listen. As I listen, God talks to me. There is never any monotony or boredom when communicating with God. Even the most trivial thoughts expressed become very enthusiastic and exciting when God is part of the conversation. I pray in English. I pray in tongues. God always speaks to me "in my understanding" (1 Corinthians 14:13, NASB). That is, I always easily understand what He says to me. In casual conversation, God will often use what I call "Okie talk." He speaks to me in Oklahoma slang—Okie talk.

One day, I was on a trip to Denver, Colorado, then to Amarillo, Texas, and finally back home to Tulsa, Oklahoma. As I traveled west on Interstate 70 in Western Kansas, I was praying constantly. Out there, you see miles and miles, hours and hours of flat country with wheat fields intermingled with cow pasture. The drive gets monotonous.

As the afternoon sun was getting close to the horizon, I passed the exit to Colby, Kansas. In another five miles was a roadside rest area. I slowed to exit there for a "pit stop." Parking in a designated truck area, I noticed a young Black lady sitting on the hood of an older model car. I asked if she was having mechanical trouble. She replied, "No, we are out of gas. My husband has gone back to Colby to buy gas." I had passed a young Black man walking along the highway carrying a one-gallon milk jug full of gasoline. As I left the interstate rest area, I was praying for the couple. Within a mile, it was clear to me that God wanted me to help the young people. Checking to make sure there was no close traffic in either direction "I shot a quick U-turn" on a paved crossover reserved for state highway maintenance vehicles. (Please don't tell Mr. Hoffmeier or the Highway Police.) Heading back east, I saw a vehicle stopping to give the man a ride. I made another U-turn, this time legal at the Colby exit, and returned to the rest area.

As I talked with the man, I explained that I wanted to be of assistance to them, but when leaving my Tulsa truck terminal, I had overlooked the need to get expense money for the three-day trip. I could not give them cash expense money, having only $12 cash with me. "Have you had anything to eat this evening?" His reply was, "We are okay. We have some apples that we have eaten today." He also explained that their destination was Denver, where he had a job waiting for him. But they had run out of gas and money. It was another two hundred miles to Denver, and that one-gallon jug of gas might get them only fifteen miles—in the dark! I told them, "I don't have money, but what I do have, I will give you. In my truck is a large cooler with plenty of ham, cheese, lettuce, mayonnaise, and rye bread. I will give each of you one of the best freshly made sandwiches on this highway."

We were having an interesting conversation as they hungrily ate the sandwiches. I knew of an all-night truck stop a few miles farther west. There, I bought them a full tank of gas using my company fuel card. I could reimburse the company when I returned to Tulsa. Now they could get to Denver and his new job. The young couple was very grateful.

At the truck stop, the man graciously thanked me for the sandwiches and gas. I confronted him with a statement intended for its shock value. I was sure it would catch the full attention of them both. "Everything has its price. I have given you food and gas, but there is a price to pay." The young Black man reacted fully ready to defend the honor and integrity of his young and attractive wife against this "lecherous, deceiving White man." I quickly continued, "What I want is five minutes of your time. During those five minutes, I want to talk to you about Jesus and going to heaven. If you are willing, let's go into the café. I will buy coffee for the three of us. If you are not comfortable with doing that, you are free to go on to Denver." He was not only shocked but also amazed. They looked at each other, made a couple of comments to each other, turned to me, and happily agreed to spend a few minutes with me. They went to park their car. I went into the café. This gave them an opportunity to "skip out on me" if they truly did not trust me.

By the time the coffee was served, the couple was at my table with smiles on their faces. We talked about their spiritual lives and salvation. They both were clear about their salvation, assuring me that they both had accepted Jesus as their personal Lord and Savior. They were unsure of going to heaven because of sin in their lives, both past and present. As a minister, I find that uncertainty is common among Christians. We discussed their spiritual beliefs and lives. I gave them scriptures to support what they had told me about their commitment to Jesus and God. I also gave them scriptures concerning assurance that they would go to heaven and not hell. For privacy, we went outside. I prayed with them for their love for God, love for each of the three of us, and God's love for each of us. Then, I prayed for forgiveness of sins, strength to live a Christian life, and safety on their trip. Next, I prayed for success in the new job and health and prosperity in their lives.

As we parted, they were excited and happy. Their gas tank was full. Their tummies were full, and their spirits were full.

It was difficult to determine who was the most blessed, them or me. As I drove on toward my destination, I was reflecting on the time and evening events with this young couple. These scriptures came to me. "It is more blessed to give than to receive." Acts 20:35, James 1:22–27, and James 2:14–22 (NASB), "Faith without works is dead."

I thanked God for the opportunity to serve Him "from the seat of the truck" by blessing the young couple. I also prayed blessings of success and prosperity for Mr. Hoffmeier and his trucking company. Clearly, God was using me as an evangelist. It was just not in the manner that I expected. All of this seemed like normal happening as I stepped out in faith. That evening, I had ministered to "one or two." It would be about two to three years later that God would reveal to me these events as part of Phase 5 of my training for the ministry.

Traveling on I-44 approaching Springfield, Missouri, traffic became slow. The Highway Patrol had a van stopped. Five patrol cars surrounded the van. "A drug bust?" I never found out.

When we finally got through Springfield on the open road, I passed some slower-moving trucks. One of them had a lady driver. At a normal quick glance, as I passed, I noticed her hair was cut short and neatly combed. It appeared that she had just enough makeup on to enhance her natural features. I picked up the CB mic and said, "This is the Miracle Man in the tanker truck that just passed you. It sure is encouraging to see a lady driver with her hair fixed and looking neat. I have noticed that many lady drivers neglect their appearance when on the road."

"Oh, hi, Miracle Man. I like to keep myself as neat as possible when working." We had a few minutes of casual, pleasant conversation.

I asked, "What is your handle?"

Her reply was, "Sweet Angel."

I commented, "I like that handle. It has a good connotation. How did you get that handle?"

"Some of the drivers that I work with gave it to me." As the conversation continued, her comments rapidly became crude and sometimes indecent. She talked about going into bars and "picking up" unknown men to spend the night with. Also, her two boys from a previous marriage were commented on. This provided my opening for Christian witnessing to Sweet Angel.

"You speak very strongly about your love for your two young boys. I am a preacher. Maybe I can offer some suggestions to make life a little happier for you."

"Ha ha ha, men have been lying to me all my life. Now, you tell me that you are a preacher. Ha ha ha. I had a man tell me vulgar and inappropriate comments. Then, when I got him in bed, he wasn't even near the sexually virile man that he boasted to be." She began to blurt out over the CB some of the most vulgar jokes that I remember hearing. By this time, I was fifty years old and had heard enough crude and vulgar jokes that I thought I probably had heard a few of the worst. But "Sweet Angel" was being vulgarly creative with some of her jokes, over the air, with no apparent shame or embarrassment.

As she talked, I kept searching for some way, something to say to effectively influence her. I asked the Holy Spirit several times during this conversation, "What can I tell Sweet Angel that will catch her attention and minister to her?" Nothing came to me.

Sweet Angel's truck had a governor on the motor that limited speed. After a few minutes, I said, "Sweet Angel, I have to make some time, so I am going to speed up and leave you. By the way, what does your handle mean?"

"I don't know. You tell me what it means. You said you are a preacher."

"I will have to give that some thought. Hope to see you down the road."

"Okay, Miracle Man, have a safe trip."

When I got out of CB range, I began to pray. "Holy Spirit, I have questions. Why did You not answer me, or why could I not hear Your answers as I talked with Sweet Angel? If I see her again, what will I effectively minister to her? Please create an opportunity for me to minister to her."

The Holy Spirit spoke clearly into my spirit, "As you talked to her, you were distracted by her comments and could not hear Me. Her handle, 'Sweet Angel,' is a contradiction in terms. She is anything but a sweet angel! When you see her again, tell her about the basic promises of God, which are love, joy, peace, health, and prosperity. If she accepts Jesus as her Lord and Savior, these character qualities will develop in her life. But she must make a strong commitment to Jesus and be willing for her entire life to change."

Five hours later, I had crossed Eastern Missouri on I-44 and traveled ninety miles through Illinois to stop at the city of Effingham for lunch and fuel. There are three major truck stops in Effingham. After about a one-hour break, with both a full tummy and fuel tank, I pulled out on Interstate 70 and dropped behind an Olympic Express truck. This was the company Sweet Angel drove for. I said, "Sweet Angel, is that you ahead of the Miracle Man?" With excitement, she replied, "Yes, Miracle Man. I am surprised to hear from you again."

In three more miles, the Interstate Highway divided. I was to take I-70 east to Cincinnati. She told me that she was taking I-57 north to Chicago. I got right to the point. "Sweet Angel, after I left you, I prayed for you. The Holy Spirit said to tell you that if you want a lifetime of happiness, then find a preacher or go to a church and accept Jesus as your Lord and Savior. If you do this, your whole life will change. The basic promises of God for His people will develop in your life. The result will be love, joy, peace, health, and prosperity like you have never experienced before."

By this time, I was headed east, and she was headed north, her voice getting weaker as we were reaching the maximum CB range. "Okay, Miracle Man, I will give that some serious thought. See you down the road."

I have never seen nor talked to Sweet Angel again. The Holy Spirit answered my prayer and created the opportunity for me to "witness with power" to her (Acts 1:8). He had shown me again that He is personal and would speak both to me and through me.

Since that encounter, I have consistently used the phrase "Basic promises of God, love, joy, peace, health, and prosperity" when preaching from the pulpit and witnessing one-on-one. Previously, I had never put those five terms together. Checking my

Bible, I was quickly assured that the statement was scriptural truth. I will continue to use the statement.

The Holy Spirit of God had once more used me to minister in an unusual evangelistic manner. Plus, He had taught me that even in my serious and conscientious efforts to witness to the unsaved, I could get distracted and fail. I had to fully depend on Him. He is the Spirit of Truth, and He speaks for the Father.

> But when He, the Spirit of Truth [the truth-giving Spirit] comes, He will guide you into all the truth [the whole, full truth]. For He will not speak His own message [on His own authority]; but He will tell you whatever He hears [from the Father; He will give the message that has been given to Him] and He will announce and declare to you the things that are to come [that will happen in the future].
>
> — John 16:13 (AMP)

Late one night, I had unloaded the tanker at an oil refinery in Markus Hook, Pennsylvania. Bordering the refinery on the east side was the Delaware River. On the south side of the refinery was a fence bordering the state of Delaware. The refinery had been built many years ago when a "big" truck had only one load axle and the trailer only one load axle. The total length of the truck and trailer would be about thirty to forty feet. Today's trucks have two load axles and two load axles on the tanker trailer. The total length is now closer to sixty-five to seventy feet.

Maneuvering through the refinery, with its narrow lanes and ninety-degree corners, was extremely difficult. This required men "spotters" both front and back to avert accidents. My truck-driving skills were severely tested that night.

Ready to leave after loading a different product for another distant location, I pulled across the scales to weigh. This done, I moved into a parking area, so other trucks had access to the scales. Inside the scale shack, I was filling out the necessary paperwork and needed to know the date. I asked if there was a calendar in the room. Another driver, whose truck was now on the scales, said, "I will give you a pocket calendar. Be sure to read the back of the calendar card." He then hot-footed out the door. I looked at the reverse side of the card. Printed on it was the plan of salvation. I quickly realized that he was a Christian who wanted to witness but did not have the courage to do so. After all, many times, a person gets rejected, sometimes harshly, when attempting to witness for Christ. I left my paperwork on the counter and ran out the door to catch the driver. As he was putting his truck in gear, I jumped up on the running board and strongly said through the open window, "Hey, fella, if you are going to give me something like that calendar, you could at least take time to explain the message on the back!"

He was obviously apprehensive, wanting to get out of there and away from me. We were talking through his open truck window, our faces hardly two feet apart. He wanted to leave, but I would not get off his truck. With a softened tone of voice, I asked some leading questions, making it easy for him to reply.

He gave scripturally sound responses to my questions. I asked more questions, drawing God's Word out of him. He began to relax and gave easily understood answers and explanations to the plan of salvation message on the back of the card. As we talked, I consciously encouraged the driver with my altered attitude and questions.

Finally, I told the man that I was an evangelist, had been to Bible school, and knew all that he had explained to me. Using scripture and comments appropriate to my purpose, I did all I could to strengthen and encourage the driver to step out with boldness and confidence as he witnessed to people for Jesus. The man was very open and receptive. Seeing another truck approaching the scales, I briefly prayed for the driver and went back inside to complete my paperwork.

If you, the reader, wonder if this manner of witnessing was appropriate, my defense is this: it worked! It was effective. Never before or since that incident have I witnessed quite like that. Was it scripturally appropriate to do what I did on this occasion? I refer you to Acts 4:28–31: "Peter and John were filled with the Spirit and spoke with boldness and confidence" (author's paraphrase). With the hours that I prayed each day as I drove along the highway, I definitely was "filled with the Spirit and spoke with boldness and confidence." Clearly, I was being led by the Holy Spirit. Even for me, this was not a normal style of witnessing. To me, being led by the Spirit is normal. It is a lifestyle. Galatians 5:25 (NASB) states, "If we live by the Spirit, let us also walk by the Spirit."

A pastor in my home area taught a series titled "The Seven Styles of Evangelism." One of these lessons was "The Confrontational Style of Evangelism." This pastor had sat within easy sight and hearing distance from me in the Bogota, Colombia, airport at 5:30 a.m. We were waiting to catch our plane flight to Tulsa, Oklahoma. He observed and listened as I witnessed to a Japanese lady seated next to me. She said her religion was Buddhism. As I confronted her with truths concerning Jesus and salvation, she readily accepted. My wife, Linda, and I prayed with the Japanese lady for her salvation right then and there. Later, in his teaching sermon, the pastor stated, "The person that I know who uses the confrontational style of evangelism most effectively is Jerry Clark!"

God spoke to me during a time of prayer in 1992. He said, "Confront the issue, not the person." I have never forgotten that statement. With the Japanese lady, I had confronted the issue of Buddhism and Christianity. She understood and was not offended or upset. With the frightened truck driver, I had confronted the issue of his fear, not the man. He received. Like the Japanese lady, he obviously was a changed person. "You shall go speak. You shall speak to one or two, four or five…"

With the many accounts described of how the Holy Spirit worked through me, you, the reader, may question, "Did Jerry ever miss hearing from the Holy Spirit?" Was Jerry always obedient to do what the Holy Spirit commanded, or as is so often the case, gently spoke? If I ever missed hearing from the Holy Spirit when He spoke to me, I was not aware of it. Of course, I would not be aware if I did not hear Him. Was I always obedient to do what I heard? Only once have I been disobedient. That was because of procrastination, not refusal to do what He told me.

Late one night, probably 1:00 a.m., I was sitting in the café of a major truck stop in San Antonio, Texas. I had struggled to stay awake during the last hour on the highway. I had not eaten an evening meal, so I was very hungry, also. I had eaten tasty meals at this truck stop during past trips, so I was anxious to get there where ample parking was available for 18-wheel trucks. I was looking forward to a good meal and a night's rest in the sleeper cab of my truck after the meal.

I parked the truck, heaving a sigh of relief, then walked into the café. The coffee was hot and refreshing as I waited a few minutes for the meal. Fighting sleep and exhaustion, I began to eat when the meal was set before me. Across the aisle sat another driver in a booth by himself. The Holy Spirit spoke to me very clearly and said, "Go to that driver's booth and tell him that whatever questions he has concerning God and the Bible, you have the answers for him." I replied, "Okay, I will do that."

Many people would be shocked and overwhelmed to hear a command of that nature. They might have questions such as "How can I know all the answers to all the questions a person might ask concerning the Bible? Who am I to think that I could answer any question that an unknown person might ask?"

It was not me, but God working through me, that would enable me to accomplish what God wanted. I did not have to have superior knowledge and abilities. Rather, I merely needed to be obedient to God!

Moses questioned his abilities when God spoke to him and told him, "You will lead My people out of captivity in Egypt." When Moses accepted God's call on his life, God performed miracles through him (Exodus Chapter 3).

Gideon questioned his abilities when God called him into His service. When he accepted God's call on his life, God performed miracles through Gideon (Judges Chapter 6).

So, did I have the answer to any question that this truck driver might ask? *No!* All I needed to do was be sensitive and obedient to the Holy Spirit within me. He would give me the answers to the man's questions. If God chooses to do miracles of any nature through me, it will be up to Him, not me.

As I sat eating the delicious food, relaxing, and gaining strength, I was also contemplating the possible results of the conversation. I knew by God's Spirit within me that the man had serious, life-changing questions if he could only find the answers. Working through me, God was about to reveal this man's answers. As I was finishing my meal, I glanced toward his booth. The man was gone! I hastily got up and walked to the cash register area. He was not there. I also looked in the convenience store area and the men's room. No driver. He was gone. I had missed the opportunity to serve God in a supernatural manner and bless the man. What a tragedy! How discouraging! How frustrating this was for me! Some six years previously, I had made a deep, heartfelt commitment to God. "God, I will go anywhere You want me to go and do anything that You want me to do. I will say anything that You want me to say to anybody at any time. Just make your message clear to me so I don't miss You." God had made His message clear to me, but because of my physical fatigue, I had not been obedient when

I needed to. Timing is critical. God had already given me one memorable lesson concerning timing in 1983. That testimony is in Phase 1 of this book.

Being extremely tired and sleepy was no excuse. I had heard from the Holy Spirit. Even though I was going to be obedient in action, I was disobedient in timing. I had missed the opportunity to serve God in a supernatural manner and bless the driver.

As I contemplated the situation, all I knew to do was beg God's forgiveness for my disobedience to His timing. I repented, then forgave myself. I also renewed my vow of obedience to God. What is left to do, then? Even though the memory of the timing mistake still bothered me, I went on with my life of serving my living God, knowing that God is quick to forgive. When He forgives, He chooses not to remember our sins (Isaiah 43:25). God does not hold grudges. I was in His good graces again. Hebrews 4:16 (NASB) states, "Let us therefore draw near with confidence to the throne of grace, that we may receive mercy and may find grace to help in our time of need."

During the two years of cross-country truck driving and ministering in many and unique ways, there were also many, many other situations where God used me. Some of those situations were notable. Some of the types of situations had become routine and normal. I have recorded only a few of the more prominent events. Possibly, in a future book, I will relate testimonies of the "lot lizards," prostitutes who worked the truck-stop parking lots and highway rest areas. Then, there were pastors who admitted to me after a service that the Holy Spirit had told them to allow me to preach. Whatever their varied excuses were, they were disobedient to the Holy Spirit and refused. It was an exciting part of life. The lessons learned, I still use today, some thirty-two years later.

Phase 6
Ministering in a Church

During the two-year cross-country truck driving phase of training, I occasionally had the opportunity to preach in churches in a typical Sunday or midweek service. At the time, I was not aware that God was putting me through various phases of training for the ministry. I thought I was already in the ministry, just not full-time. I was clear that He had called me to minister, and I was very anxious to do so on a full-time basis. At every opportunity, I would minister wherever I could in whatever capacity was available. Sometimes, when visiting a church, the pastor would ask me to give a two-to-five-minute "word of encouragement." Often, this was a spur-of-the-moment invitation. Always, I went to a church spiritually prepared. That is, I was "prayed up and read up." I always asked the Holy Spirit to provide an opportunity to speak or help the pastor minister in some capacity. He often provided the opportunity.

When these impromptu invitations came, I did not have a formally prepared statement to make. Rather, I would ask the Holy Spirit what to say. Each time during the walk from my seat to the front of the church, the Holy Spirit would give me a brief message. At first, I would pray quietly and desperately as I walked to the front. As I became aware that the Holy Spirit was faithful to give me messages consistently, I became more confident in hearing from Him. He was and is diligent in speaking through me.

I spoke with a pastor acquaintance in Mesa, Arizona. We arranged a date to minister in his church. When the date came, the meeting went well. The Holy Spirit moved with His gifts. The congregation was open and receptive. The pastor and I discussed the possibility of me coming to work with him in his church as an evangelist. Later, I took Linda and our two youngest teenage children on a visit to Mesa. I wanted them to view the situation and for all of us to be in agreement about the possibility of quitting our jobs, moving 1,100 miles, and working in a church.

Our oldest daughter, Wanda, now grown, was living in Albuquerque, NM. Our second daughter, Cheryl, was attending Oral Roberts University, Tulsa, OK. Our son, Paul, was scheduled to graduate from high school that spring and had his own plans for his immediate future, independent of us. Our youngest daughter, Janice, still had two years of high school to complete. Linda and I were aware of her active involvement in school and church activities. I particularly was not aware of her strong leadership roles and the influence that this petite sixteen-year-old girl was having on her peers. Even in discussions with Janice, I was not conscious of the depth of the impact that she was having on her peer groups and adult leaders or sponsors.

As time progressed, various details were worked out, and the discussions concerning the move continued. Janice strongly preferred to stay in Chelsea, Oklahoma, where we lived, but accepted that if it was God's will for our lives, then she must come into agreement with us. Naturally, a lot of praying by each of us was taking place. We wanted to be certain that we were within God's will.

Linda and I combined our last paychecks with our savings account and paid all current bills. We rented a moving truck, "loaded all our earthly possessions," and moved the 1,100 miles to Mesa, Arizona. In one of the discussions with the pastor, we were discussing moving expenses, a place to rent, and other pertinent subjects. He made the statement, "I will help you with the move." I thought that when we arrived, he would have a list of apartments and houses for us to consider renting. I also thought that he would have a salary plan commensurate with our church ministry responsibilities that we discussed in his office when we made the commitment to move there. After arriving, the pastor made it clear that none of that was available: "I did not say that." Thinking back to the discussions, I realized that He only implied or alluded to helping us. There was no definite commitment from him. This pastor had manipulated me into a big and expensive move with a strong ministry commitment, but I ended up paying all the expenses. What a discouraging, frustrating disappointment that was!

During a previous trip to Mesa, I had met the church youth minister and his visiting parents. The father and I discussed a three-week construction-maintenance job that was scheduled to start June 1 at a location about two hours west of Mesa. The company needed extra labor. The father assured me of a job for both my son and me. The hourly pay was good, and we would be working seven twelve-hour days each week. This short job would give Linda and me a financial boost to start life in Arizona. After the job completion, our son would return to Oklahoma and pursue his life independently of us.

Our son and I parked the moving truck at a safe location in Mesa. We drove his car to the motel about one hour west of Mesa, where the construction crew was staying. We got a quick one-hour nap in the car. When the crew loaded in the crew bus, we went to work with them. Twelve hours of labor in the one-hundred-and-ten-degree Arizona sun after driving all the previous day and night was severely taxing on us physically. But we survived.

Fortunately, I had a few days' grace on the truck rental. The first evening after work, we showered, ate supper, then collapsed in bed. The night's rest was a lifesaver. Renting an apartment and unloading the truck would have to wait. The following evening after work, we drove to the church and met with the pastor. I expected him to have a volunteer crew from the church to help unload the truck the following night. I was completely depleted of cash, so I asked for a salary advance to get us by until the first job payday. The pastor's response to my questions was, "I don't know who we can get to work at night to unload the truck. You are not on salary, and I do not have money to advance you. What an opportunity you have to make your faith in God work for your finances." I replied, "I have plenty of faith in God for finances and other needs. But I have used all my money to get here. I need cash for food until payday."

"Well, let's pray and believe God that He will supply your needs. Here, I have some change in this drawer. You can have that." He gave me the $26 of loose change. A big red flag went up! *What have I gotten myself into?*

I managed to find a suitable apartment and arranged the rent payment. The next night, three men from the church helped my son and me unload the moving truck. After working twelve hours in the one-hundred-and-ten-degree hot sun, driving forty-five miles, and unloading the truck, we caught a few hours of sleep. We were exhausted! Somehow, we managed to keep our attitudes positive. God had to be instilling supernatural strength and endurance into us. It certainly was not our natural strength that sustained us.

The job superintendent proved to be compassionate and gave us a pay advance. Now we had meal money until payday.

Several days later, the pastor called me at the motel. "We have a state ministry convention to host at our church. I am the state director of the ministry organization. God has spoken to me that you are the man to organize the convention."

I responded, "I have no experience with this type of job responsibility. Are you sure that you have heard from God?"

"Oh yes. I definitely have. You are the appointed man."

I asked, "When is this convention?"

"Thirty days from now! Come by my office. I have a convention organization manual. You can follow its plan, and everything will work out."

Although I was unhappy with and privately questioned several of his decisions so far, I still had confidence in the pastor. He was aware of my background experience as a public school teacher and high school principal. I considered that possibly he thought that because of that background and with evaluation of other congregation leaders I was the best qualified among the congregation to organize and be the convention director. In conversation, he agreed with that evaluation. He also assured me that he had heard from God, and I was to be the convention director.

After much, much prayer, Linda and I were comfortable that we had heard from God concerning the move to Mesa. We are very strong about commitment. We were fully committed, and a few unexpected decisions and problems or obstacles were not going to change our commitment. With serious questions in mind about how to organize a state convention in only thirty days, I reluctantly agreed to accept the responsibility of state convention director. I drove the forty-five miles to the church and picked up the manual. The pastor did his best to give me encouraging "faith-filled comments."

This project was going to take a lot of prayer, and God was going to have to direct every step of the entire project. I sure did not know how to plan and implement a state convention, especially with only thirty days to organize it. I had to hear from God about every detail!

The next morning, due to unexpected circumstances on the job, several of the crew, including me, did not go to work. We were told about the circumstances just before loading the crew bus at about 5:00 a.m. Most of the men went back to bed. I went outside and walked the desert where we were staying at Goodyear, Arizona, west of Phoenix.

For one and a half hours, I walked, prayed, listened, asked questions, and intently concentrated on hearing from God about how to organize the state convention. God is faithful and gracious. He laid out the entire organizational plan in detail. As I talked to God, He would speak into my spirit very clearly and distinctly.

Next, I went to the motel, opened the two-inch-thick convention planning manual, and "devoured" the information in four hours. That, in itself, was supernatural. Then, I drove the forty-five miles to the church and started implementing the plan step by step as God had directed me. Two young adult lady church members I met at the church assured me they were willing and capable of taking very responsible positions that required much skilled work. A young man briefly visiting me from nearby Phoenix had an advertising degree. He organized a brochure. By the end of the week, brochures were printed, and invitations were mailed. Speakers had been contacted, and their commitments were received and scheduled. All the details were falling into place. By the end of the second week, the primary part of the work was complete. Many members of the church readily gave their support. *Praise God!* His plan was working as only He could make it work.

Approximately three hundred people from across the state of Arizona registered and attended the convention. Hopefully, expecting only one hundred attendees, we were pleasingly overwhelmed. The numbers far exceeded our expectations. The entire program was a success. *Praise God again!*

The last event was a formal luncheon. Speakers and all others involved in the organization and work to make the convention a success were invited. Approximately ninety to one hundred people attended. The pastor, primary convention speaker, and state officers were seated at the speaker's table. As state convention director, naturally, I expected one of those seats. Instead, the pastor assigned me to a table at the far end of the room close to the back door! I was shocked! Was I a part of the church ministry, or just another worker without a salary and obviously no recognition? It was apparent that the pastor wanted all recognition and certainly was not going to recognize or promote me in any manner. I questioned the situation but did not complain. This was the pastor's first church, so I gave him the benefit of the doubt concerning how he managed or mismanaged me and my position as an evangelist working in the church.

This was the completion of the first month of working in this church. With everything that had happened concerning me, the church, and my relationship with the pastor, I began to pray: "God, what is going on here? The pastor treats me like he does not want me here unless there is something important to be done that nobody else can or will do. He has not paid me anything nor found me any place to preach as he promised he would. There are so many negative things happening that I am wondering if I missed hearing from You and should not be here. In a full month, there has been no income at all from this church. The relationship with church members is very good, but not so with the pastor. Should I leave?"

The pastor made it definitely clear to me that "this is my church, and you or no one else is going to make any management decisions." It was my plan and purpose to work with the pastor in his church. I would do the work of an evangelist. I planned to speak and do the work of an evangelist in other churches as that could be arranged with their pastors. The pastor had made it clear that I was not on salary. It was necessary for me to preach in other churches both to be of service to them and benefit from the financial income. The pastor had persuaded me to let him contact other pastors and arrange for me to serve them, too. "You are new here and are not acquainted with the churches and their pastors. I am established here, know the pastors, and can find you places to preach." This sounded reasonable to me, so I agreed. In nine months of serving in that church, he never found me one place to preach! I had no ministry income! His excuse, or stated reasoning, was, "I do not trust you. I do not know what you might say."

I began to pray more consistently and intently about leaving that ministry situation. God had made it clear to me that I was to go there. I was certain that He would tell me when to leave.

The pastor wanted to have a Bible school sponsored by the church. Since I had previous experience as a public high school principal, he persuaded me to organize the school. This included writing a curriculum, assigning trained and knowledgeable teachers, and all the many other phases of organizing and operating a Christian school for adults. It was a very responsible and time-consuming job. A percentage of student tuition was to be paid to me as a salary. I never received any income from that source, either. We operated the school for about six months. The small number of student enrollees was enthused, and so were the four instructors. The school was showing strong signs of initial success. This was September. I had been there since June 1, about four months. With no pay and increasing efforts by the pastor to dominate and control me, it was easy to see that this was not working out.

By July 1, I had been praying with increasing intent for God to release me from that commitment. Eventually, it became a daily request. Each time, God would tell me "No," or I did not recognize any answer in my spirit. Linda and I kept working in the church and taking care of our various responsibilities. The situation kept getting worse. Linda and I had a strong commitment to God to minister wherever and however He directed us. We are not quitters.

Linda and I were assigned the task of delivering meals prepared by church members to other church members who were sick or temporarily homebound. We were to deliver the meal, explaining that the food was from the church, as directed by the pastor. Also, we were to pray or minister to the sick person according to our perception of their needs. This worked out very well for us. We enjoyed this type of ministry. After all, God had told me to "go speak. Speak to one or two, four or five…" This type of ministry was distinctly within our evangelistic calling. Knowing how sensitive the pastor was that he received recognition from the sick people for the meals, we were careful to state that he had sent us. Apparently, we were being too effective with the one-on-one ministry when praying for and sharing God's Word as we delivered food. Possibly, compliments or praise of our work had been received by the pastor. I was called into his office and reprimanded strongly for drawing attention and recognition to myself instead of giving him credit with the food recipients. "You are not the pastor. I am." He and I were both strong-willed and outspoken, so the discussion became "hot."

"God, when are You going to let me out of this mess?"

During the previous summer, the youth minister had taken a group of thirty to forty teenagers to summer camp for a few days. The youth minister had planned well, and the results were outstanding. Several teenagers received salvation, were baptized in the Holy Spirit, and had wonderful, exciting spiritual experiences. Their testimonies in church were tremendous. The youth group increased in number. This large group required more expenses to operate. For whatever the stated reason by the pastor, expense money was reduced rather than being increased. Eventually, the youth minister resigned. He could no longer afford to live on the meager salary now paid by the church. I noticed that with his success ministering to the youth, he received very much recognition and respect. Soon, his area of ministry was suspended, and he had to leave the church.

Looking at my own situation, I saw there had been a commendable success with the state convention and the first few months of the Bible school. Our other responsibilities had brought Linda and me recognition, respect, and popularity within the church congregation. Suppression of my leadership efforts by the pastor had been developing since the first success and was getting worse.

In my formal education, I earned a bachelor's degree and master's degree plus twenty-four semester hours in public school education. In addition, I earned a degree from Rhema Bible Training School, Broken Arrow, Oklahoma. The pastor did not have a college degree; he had attended but not completed the same Bible school. He was determined to be in dominant control of me and everyone else in that church. I had come there to work with him to help build his church, not be dominated by him.

"God, when are You going to release me from this unbearable situation?"

One of the weekly responsibilities that he gave me was to wash the church van. From my viewpoint, this was ridiculous. Was I being arrogant? Absolutely not! From a management viewpoint, you do not send your most qualified leadership person to do a task that any volunteer with a driver's license could handle.

"God, how much longer do I have to tolerate this situation? I want out of here!"

How did we survive financially for nine months working full-time in the church with no church income? Linda had a schoolteacher's degree with eighteen years of experience. She earned some money each month for substitute teaching in the local public schools. Occasionally, she and I picked up a few dollars doing temporary odd jobs. Occasionally, the church gave us a sack of groceries.

I daily passed a small acreage owned by the city. It had a communications tower and water well on the property. Formerly, the acreage was part of an orchard. The land was overgrown with high grass and weeds. Oranges and grapefruit were falling on the ground and rotting. I began to scavenge the still-edible fruit. The tasty fruit was added to our meals and sometimes served as full meals. The fruit was nutritious, and I lost fifteen pounds, yet I had energy.

"God, when is this going to end? I thought my tolerance peak would have ended long ago. But here I am, still waiting to hear from You. I have tolerated this situation far longer than I ever thought that I could or would. When can I leave? Why can't I leave?"

There are many more of these types of circumstances that could be told. But this shall suffice. I was doing all that I knew to do to protect Linda and Janice from my own discontent and many of the negative details of the circumstances.

One of the things that I did that became common was help people move. I had furniture loading and moving experience from working for DTL Movers when attending Rhema, so my moving skills and knowledge were often utilized. A single lady with three young children in the church needed to move. I enlisted the assistance of a strong and willing young man in the church. We borrowed another church member's pickup truck and sixteen-foot trailer. Early one morning we drove to her house, loaded all her furniture and other possessions, then left town to drive to her new house location.

We had driven only two to three miles when I clearly and distinctly heard the voice of God in my spirit. God said, "Get your finances in order and be ready to move." That excited me so much that I had to grip the steering wheel tightly to keep from jumping out of the moving pickup. I had been praying daily, intently, sometimes desperately, for months, asking God to release me from that church. He had finally spoken and relieved me of the commitment and responsibilities. It was His timing, not mine. I would have left seven to eight months before.

So as not to attract the attention of the lady and man riding with me, I spoke to God from my spirit. "God, what in the world have I been doing here these past nine months? This looks like a total disaster for me from every viewpoint." God spoke to me again: "You have been learning how not to minister! This has been another phase of your training."

"Phase of training! God, I thought I was already in the ministry. How many phases of training have I been through?"

"Count them up." Immediately, I knew how many phases of ministry training God had put me through. I also knew distinctly what each phase was and when each started and ended. I had just completed Phase 6. I asked, "How many more phases do I have to go through before I am finally in the full-time ministry?"

God replied, "How many is completion?" I knew that the biblical number for completion was seven. *Oh, I have one more phase of training before God puts me in full-time ministry. For the past nine years, God has been training me. It has been both formal schooling and "on-the-job" training. I wonder what the next phase will be and when it will start and end. Then, exactly what style will my evangelism ministry consist of? Exactly what does God have planned for me? What is the resulting purpose of this many years of unusual training?* My curiosity was almost as strong as the excitement caused by God speaking to me.

The next morning, in front of several church workers, I told the pastor that God had spoken to me, and we were leaving "his" church. This caused a strong emotional upset with him. I had expected that, so I was prepared for his reaction. I gathered my personal belongings and left the building.

Linda has always had an unusually strong commitment to God. Initially, she questioned my decision to leave the church. When I received a phone call at home from the pastor, she was close enough to overhear the conversation, including his personal physical threats directed at me. That eliminated her doubts about my decision to leave that ministry.

We started preparing to move the 1,100 miles back to Oklahoma. The construction-maintenance company that I had worked for the previous summer had another phase of work starting in only a few weeks. Again, working seven twelve-hour days per week allowed me to make enough money to pay all local financial bills and immediate moving expenses. After the job ended, we rented a storage unit for our furniture, packed Janice's small car with each of our personal needs, and traveled back to Oklahoma. We arrived at our son's one-bedroom apartment with a total of $35 in our pockets. He worked nights, so Linda and I slept in the bed. When Paul came in from his night job, we got up so he could have the bed to sleep.

Yes, we had learned a strong lesson about "how not to minister."

Phase 7
Pastoring a Church

Transition—Time of Change: What Do We Do Now?

Pray and take action. Linda walked the short distance across a nearby shopping center parking lot. She applied for and received a minimum-wage-paying job. Naturally, with her education and teaching experience, she would have preferred a "position" with much better pay. But the $35 was dwindling fast. We both needed a job quickly. Using Paul's car as he slept, I looked for work. With my varied job skills, I began looking for almost any work that would provide immediate income. I kept my basic carpentry tools in Paul's car. This consisted of a power skill saw, drill, level, square, and pencil. If any type of wood maintenance or construction work appeared, I was prepared right then. In a few weeks, we managed to purchase a good-quality used pickup truck. This was an asset to my odd jobs and provided independent transportation for Linda and me. We were surviving financially but needed to do far more than just survive.

One day, Linda asked, "If money were not a factor, what would you do?"

I thought only a minute or so. "I would find a pipeline construction job. On those jobs, the hourly pay is good, and they typically work sixty or more hours per week, so the overtime pay is good."

She replied, "Find a pipeline job!"

I had been away from that type of work for several years and had lost all contacts. How do I find where a pipeline job is or will soon start? Checking pipeline construction trade magazines, I found there were three major jobs planned for the near future in the northwest New Mexico-Arizona area. One was to start construction within one to two months.

In a conversation concerning finding a pipeline job, I said, "Linda, if I did what I really want to do, we would go to Gallup, New Mexico, where that first pipeline job is scheduled to start. Every morning, I would be on the job talking to the 'Spread Man' [job superintendent] until he hired me."

Linda replied, "I'm game."

We started thinking, planning, and praying. Within a few days, a relative offered to sell us an eight by twenty-eight feet travel trailer that he had taken in on a business trade. Credit purchase arrangements were negotiated. Now we had a travel trailer to live in, a pickup to pull it with, and a possible job to go to. With some annual property rental income for expense money, we headed to New Mexico.

We stopped in Albuquerque and registered with the state's Teamsters Union. I was number thirty-four on the out-of-work list. With much prayer covering this entire adventure, God gave me a Holy Spirit-inspired Word of Knowledge (message for an individual inspired by the Holy Spirit) for the dispatcher when registering. She seemed impressed. We visited with our daughter, Wanda, who lived in Albuquerque for a few days, then pulled "our house" to the job location at

Gallup, New Mexico. Already on the job location, I could go to work at a moment's notice. I was the first person dispatched to the job from the union office. Somehow, I had jumped from number thirty-four to number one. Did God inspire this? Certainly, God had answered our prayers.

I worked the three-month job and signed up to work the following summer on a well-paying job with the same company in central Oregon. When called the following May, we pulled the travel trailer there and worked that five-month job. While waiting through the winter for the company's next job to start, I contacted a church in Seaside, Oregon. They were searching for a new pastor. After preaching for them once, they hired me. Ministering in the church full-time and not truck driving, *I was in the full-time ministry*, or so I thought.

A minister friend in Tulsa prophesied to us concerning pastoring the church at Seaside, "You are going into a mission field without support." Linda and I knew this prophet well. We had much respect for her sensitivity to the Holy Spirit and her accuracy when prophesying. For the first time, we questioned this prophecy from her. Our thinking was, "This is Oregon in the United States. Mission fields are in foreign countries." How little we knew.

After pastoring the church at Seaside, Oregon, for several months, we realized how accurate her prophecy was. Oregon, especially the Willamette Valley, where the cities of Portland, Salem, and Eugene are located, and the coastal area are full of people who are very liberal in their thinking. These areas were prominent with people who were homosexuals and "New Age" thinking. They not only resisted Christianity, but so often they fought against Christianity. This was noticeable in the news media and even from conversations in the "coffee shops." We heard one prominent pastor in Portland say, "The spirit of the northwest is a spirit of extreme independence." We received encouragement from only a few friends back home and hardly any financial support. Yes, we were "in a mission field without support."

Full time and effort were devoted to pastoring by both Linda and me. Each morning at 7:00 a.m., I went to the church to pray until 8:00 a.m. No one was there but me—and God! The first few weeks, each day, I told Him everything I knew in about ten minutes. The rest of the hour, I sat and wondered what I was doing there. Then I would walk around making an occasional comment, then wondering, "Is that God talking to me, or is it my own thinking?" I began to distinguish between my thoughts and the voice of God. After about four weeks, the hour was being filled with clearly hearing from God and talking to Him.

We began to have conversations. That was exciting. God would tell me what was going to happen in the church, who was involved, when it was going to happen, and why, and the word would be passed around that I was wrong and the other people involved were right. The events happened when and how God told me they would time after time. Leadership people were leaving. Invariably, they were "right" and "I was wrong." People would tell me, "So many people are leaving the church, and you never seem upset." I would reply, "No need for me to be upset. God told me this would happen two months ago."

The first Sunday, the supervisor for children under six years old resigned and left the church. That was a shock. People began to drop out regularly. I seriously wondered why.

I called on one of these ladies, and she told me this, "I prayed about who the new pastor would be. God told me, 'The new pastor will be a short, stocky, older man with a Southern accent.' The first Sunday you preached, I knew you were who God had spoken about." She never attended again.

A lady member called me one day and asked if I would come to her house and pray for her ten-year-old son. "He has such a severe headache that he is crying."

Linda and I went to her house. I talked to the boy for a few minutes. He became calm, and the headache left him. The lady exclaimed, "You did not pray for my son!"

I replied, "The headache left him, didn't it?"

"Yes, but you didn't pray for him!"

This lady left the church, too.

Several other people left the church for varied reasons. One lady said, "I made up my mind that I was going to leave this church before you ever came. I just wanted to stay two to three weeks to see what you were like."

Some people left because "You operate like an evangelist, not a pastor." They were referring to me being outspoken and the Holy Spirit's gifts operating through me consistently. They may have been right. We consistently had healings and other miraculous supernatural happenings that are normally consistent with the evangelist's ministry.

Another unusual obstacle was my Southern accent. I was from Oklahoma and had a definite Southern accent. It was my impression that the people in Oregon were very liberal and automatically assumed that I was prejudiced against Black people. This attitude occasionally caused dissension in the church, the community, and the general area.

I am a strong believer of God's supernatural power operating in our lives today. I expect answers to prayers. I also expect God to perform miracles as happened with the apostles in the book of Acts.

The president of the church board called me one day and asked if I would come to pray for his toes. "I have had diabetes for several years, and my blood circulation is so bad in my toes that they are turning blue-black. The doctor said he would have to amputate the toes in about three weeks. I don't want to have my toes amputated. Come pray for me." We set a time for later that day. I went to his house and asked him to sit down and remove his shoes and socks. His toes were very dark. I rubbed the toes with anointing oil, laid hands on those toes, quoted healing scriptures from the Bible, and commanded the blood vessels to open and blood to start freely flowing through his toes. Next, I thanked God for His healing power flowing into the man's feet and toes. The following Sunday at church, the man told me that he had normal color and blood circulation in his toes. God had done a healing miracle for the man.

This same man had a rather gruff, unpleasant, and conflicting personality. According to his wife, he had dominated her and was controlling in most areas of their long marriage. One Saturday night, I went walking and prayed about the church service the next day. During the prayer, God spoke to me and said, "Tell the president of the church board that if he doesn't change his attitude and start living in love, he only has months to live! If he will change his attitude or state of mind and start living in love, then he will have years to live." At the next board meeting with all five members present, I delivered that message to him. His reply was, "Well, I am seventy-seven years old, have diabetes, and am in general poor health. I don't have much longer to live anyway." We continued with the board meeting.

The following Thursday, the board president came by the church and spoke to me in his normal, harsh, surly voice and manner, "Well, I have decided to live my life in love." He then turned and left. I had heard him say the proper words, but I never received any communication of truth about living in love. He continued to live his life without any noticeable change.

About six months after I delivered the message, this man was "broad-sided" as he drove his small pickup. The pickup was damaged beyond repair. Surprisingly, he had no serious injuries. He continued to live his normal, harsh-mannered life. Eleven months after I delivered the message to him, he had a heart attack and died in his kitchen at home. God had warned him, but he would not change. He died within God's stated timing.

I received an invitation to speak to a group of forty-four people in a "homeless shelter" in nearby Astoria. They were open to receiving my message of God's personal love, inspiration, and encouragement for their individual lives. Linda and I prayed for their individual needs. In a matter of a very few weeks, we received reports of healings, people finding jobs and independent homes to live in, as well as other stated needs being met for each of the forty-four people. We considered this a supernatural happening from God.

A church member brought her twenty-eight-year-old brother to church. He was financially broke and had no place to live and no job. He was very discouraged with life. I took him under my wing. In a few weeks, he had a job, had a written financial recovery plan, and was living in a small, furnished rent house. His entire life had changed to his benefit. He also attended church regularly and followed a Bible study plan. The plan included tithing and offerings according to his income.

After a very few months, he suddenly quit attending church. A few of his friends and relatives quit church also. According to them, I had done something seriously wrong to cause these people to quit attending the church. But none of them would ever tell me why or what they believed that I had done wrong. According to them, they were right, and I was wrong. I am still puzzled about that situation.

A lady and her husband, maybe in their late forties, started attending church. She was taking several different prescription pills. Her eyes were "glassy" from the effects of the pills. After visiting with the couple in-depth several times and spending much time in prayer, I felt inspired by God to tell her, "If you will attend church consistently every Sunday morning, night, and Wednesday night, plus be diligent to follow a Bible study plan that I will write for you, then in six months' time, you will not have to take all these medicines, and you will be well. You can save the several hundred dollars per month that you are now spending on medicines."

Her reply was, "But you don't understand. The doctor said, '_____.'" She then paraphrased the doctor's comments.

I countered with, "But Jesus said, '_____.'" Then, I quoted scripture by Jesus concerning her circumstances.

Finally, I was able to persuade her to follow my plan. Within four to six months, she had eliminated the medicines, was clear-eyed, and mentally-emotionally stable.

Just a few weeks later, this same lady and her husband announced to me that "God had spoken to them." They were to move to Denver, Colorado, and enroll in a well-known and respected Bible school to prepare for the ministry. My reaction was, "That is quite commendable. I admire your desires. But you are not physically and emotionally strong enough yet. Plus, you have not studied the Bible long enough and are not sufficiently knowledgeable of God's Word to do well in a Bible school."

"Pastor Jerry, we have studied the Bible just like you told us to. We know much, much more than when we started attending church here. Besides that, God has told us to enroll at the

Bible school in Denver. It starts in only a few weeks. We must prepare to move to Denver."

"Surely, if God wants you to attend Bible school, He will tell me, your pastor, also. But He has not told me that you are to go to Bible school now."

"We are certain that we have heard from God."

"If you are certain that God spoke to you about attending Bible school, then who am I to say that He did not? I know that He has not spoken to me about you attending Bible school now."

The couple made their preparations, moved to Denver, and enrolled in Bible school. Three months later, they were back in Seaside, Oregon. The lady's eyes were glassed over with the effects of the medicines that she was taking again. Their explanation was, "After living in Seaside at ocean level, the high elevation and thin air at Denver was more than I could take. I could not breathe well there. It affected my health so bad that we had to drop out of school and move back here."

"Okay. Let's put you back on a Bible study program again and get your health rebuilt." They were willing and followed that plan. The lady's physical and emotional recovery was rapid and strong. Gradually, she was able to eliminate the medicines again.

A few months later, this same couple came to me and said, "God has spoken to us and told us to move to Seattle, Washington. We are to attend that big, well-known, and respected church there and enroll in its Bible school. To be on time there, we will be moving in a few weeks."

My reply was, "Are you certain that God has spoken to you about this move?"

"Oh yes. We have already started making plans to move and enroll there."

"I believe that it would be to your benefit to stay here and develop in your knowledge of God's Word and study how to minister. You could then enroll for the next term."

"We have heard from God. We must go now." They moved to Seattle and enrolled in the Bible school.

A few months later, we were going to be traveling through Seattle. We called this couple and arranged to have lunch and visit as we passed through. On arrival, they entertained us with a tasty meal in their home. They updated us on their Bible school training. "We both had to quit the Bible school and the church. The pastor was teaching so much biblical error that we just couldn't stay. The instructors at the Bible school were teaching so much wrong that we just could not sit in class, etc."

My reply was, "Now, wait a minute. This pastor has been preaching for over ten years. He is well-known and respected among ministers. His church has about 2,500 members. He has established a Bible school. The instructors have doctorate degrees in theology. How can the pastor and instructors be so wrong?"

"Pastor Jerry, you don't understand."

"No, I definitely do not understand!"

"The teaching and preaching were so bad we could not stay."

This couple was so definite and convinced of being "right" and everybody else being "wrong" that Linda and I finally quit attempting to minister to them. They were not members of our church anymore and we had enough problems and responsibilities within the church at home without reaching out to them long distance.

There was a family that lived about twenty-five miles out in the mountains from Seaside. They had five grown children, mostly still living at home. Occasionally, two or more of the family would attend church. But according to the entire family, I was their pastor, and River of Life Church was their church. Late one afternoon, we stopped by the church to check telephone messages. The mother, seemingly desperate, had left a phone message and asked me to call her. I called, and she quickly exclaimed, "Pastor Jerry, please pray for me. I am about to die!" Knowing she was in relatively good health, I asked, "Why do you think you are going to die?"

"I just took a whole bottle of Valium pills and washed it down with a pint of blackberry brandy!"

"Why did you do that?"

"My oldest son committed suicide this afternoon, and I am so upset. Please pray for me. I don't want to die!"

I thought, *How in the world do you pray for somebody in a situation like this? What scripture will be appropriate to use?* Mark 16:18 (NASB) came to me, "[I]f they drink any deadly poison, it shall not hurt them…" I prayed for her and then asked for directions to her house. Previously, when I asked directions to her house with the intention of making a standard "pastoral call," she could never give me clear directions, explaining, "It is too far into the mountains with too many turns, and I get confused trying to give directions." In her desperation for me to quickly drive to her house and pray for her, she instantly gave me explicit, easy-to-understand directions.

When I arrived at the house, one of the family had called a nearby rural emergency ambulance. She had been taken to the hospital in Seaside. I shared some scripture with the grown children at home, prayed for them, and then drove the twenty-five miles back to town and the hospital.

The attending doctor explained to me that they had pumped her stomach to rid it of the brandy and valium pills. They were adding liquid to her body through an IV. "She is unconscious and will wake up in the morning with a hangover headache. Other than that, she will be okay. Her husband is in the room with her. You may go in if you want to."

I entered her room and spoke to her husband. Looking at the lady, I noticed that she had obvious jerking and spasms. I told the husband that I wanted his permission to cast demons out of her, pray for her, and preach to her. He replied, "Yes, Pastor, do whatever you want."

I spoke quietly but firmly and intensely to the demons in her, commanding them to come out of her and leave the room. The spasms stopped, and an expression of peace came over her face. Then, I preached to the lady for a few minutes. Next, I prayed for her, including no hangover headache, and left the hospital.

The following morning, I visited the lady in her hospital room. She told me that she felt tired but had no headache or other discomfort. I prayed with her and some of the grown children who were in the room with her. Later that day, she was released to go home.

Another day in the life of Pastors Jerry and Linda.

One morning, about 9:30 a.m., Linda and I drove into the church parking lot. On the front church steps sat a man obviously hungover from too much alcoholic drinking the night before. When we got out of the car, he asked, "Are you the pastor?"

I replied, "Yes, I am."

"I need to talk to you."

I could see his need and replied, "Yes, you do. Come on in the church."

By this time, I had dealt with enough of the drinkers and druggies in the area that I could tell him his story just by looking at him. He was living and sleeping with his girlfriend in her mother's house. He did not have a job and was eating meals paid for by the mother and girlfriend. "Her mother treated me badly and kicked me out of the house. I have no job and no money. What am I going to do?"

I asked Linda to find some food in the church kitchen and fix him some breakfast. All that she could find was a box of spaghetti and a loaf of bread. He ate what she prepared. At least it was hot.

As she was heating the toast, I repeated his story to him as he had told me. In the conversation, I clearly and firmly pointed out his troublesome and sinful lifestyle as he had described it to me. Then, I talked to him about changing his lifestyle so that love, joy, and peace would develop. I talked to him about his salvation and his choice of going to heaven or hell. He told me that I had made it clear to him. He accepted Jesus as his personal Lord and Savior and finished his toast and spaghetti. I prayed for him, and he thanked me. Then, the young man stood up straight, shook my hand, and walked out of the church. We never saw him again.

What an unusual way to start a day.

One Wednesday evening, I started to give an opening prayer and remark. In walked a young man unknown to any of us. He took a seat and blurted out, "Do you believe in demons?"

I replied, "Yes, I do!" I could tell that he had demons in him, and as we talked, I was debating whether to cast the demons out of him right then or wait until after my lesson, then cast the demons out of him. I decided to wait. During the lesson, the man squirmed in his seat several times. He would grit and grind his teeth and occasionally speak out, often using cuss words. The demons were manifesting, causing these physical movements and expressions.

When I finished my brief lesson, I directed my attention to the young man. I spoke to the demons and commanded them to come out of him. They would not release. I worked with him for several minutes, quoting scriptures and commanding the demons to come out of him. The entire congregation of about forty people, including several young children, was praying intently in English and tongues. An older lady, very knowledgeable of the Bible, asked me to let her work with him. Her strong, powerful biblical efforts were having no effect either. Finally, she told the young man, "If you want those demons out of you, you cast them out!" He gritted and ground his teeth, then spoke very loud and strongly, "In the name of Jesus, you demons, come out of me!" The demons quickly left him. He relaxed, breathing deeply. The expression on his face changed from anger to peace.

Someone asked, "How did those demons get in you?"

This young man began his story. "I am twenty-one years old, and I am a Christian. I was saved several years ago. I questioned if demons were for real. I didn't really believe they were. One day, I decided that I would find out. I said, 'If you demons are real, come into me.' They did right then. Tonight, as I was walking down the sidewalk, the demons told me they were going to drown me in the nearby river. I was really scared. This was the first church that I came to with lights on, so I came in."

The lesson we all learned that night about interaction with demons was if a Christian invites demons into himself, he has given them authority to be there. To get the demons to leave, he must call on the authority of Jesus Himself and command the demons to leave. He gave them the freedom to inhabit his body. Only he had the authority to call on the name of Jesus to cast them out.

What an unusual way to end a day.

After several weeks of pastoring River of Life Church, Seaside Oregon, Linda and I noticed that many of the congregation had not been baptized in water. Apparently, water baptism had not been a priority with previous pastors during the approximate ten-year existence of the church. It certainly was for us. In the third chapter of Matthew, the purpose and importance of water baptism by Jesus are recorded. When asking John, the Baptist, to baptize Him, Jesus stated, "Permit it at this time;

for in this way it is fitting for us to fulfill all righteousness" (Matthew 3:15, NASB).

We began to preach and teach about the importance of water baptism. As a result, during the first-year pastoring at River of Life Church, we baptized forty-three people from a congregation of about one hundred people. We baptized people in hot tubs, a river, and anywhere we could lower people under water.

In early January, two young men visited the church. They liked what they heard and attended regularly during their three-week stay in Seaside. They were "backpacking" the West Coast. One of the men already had received his salvation. The second man received Jesus as his Lord and Savior after an altar call in an evening service. Both wanted to be baptized in water. I explained that the only place that I could baptize them was in the river that flowed past the church about fifty feet behind the building. It had snowed in the nearby mountains. The local river contained the melted snow that flowed from the mountains to the ocean. "The water is clear, cold, and about four feet deep."

"That is okay with us." We scheduled the baptism for 3:00 p.m. the next afternoon. We anticipated this to be the warmest time of this late January day.

The two men and I changed into our bathing suits in the church building, then waded into the melted snow water. A small group of church members were there in support. I quickly baptized the two young men, and we waded out of the ice-cold water. Undoubtedly, that was the quickest baptism that I ever held! We were all happy, especially after getting dry, changing into warm, dry clothes, and sipping hot chocolate.

We also taught and emphasized the importance of "baptism of the Holy Spirit." A description of this is included in Matthew Chapter 3, when Jesus was baptized in water. In verse 11, John the Baptist states, "As for me, I baptize you with water for repentance, but He who is coming after me, is mightier than I, and I am not fit to remove His sandals; He will baptize you with the Holy Spirit and fire" (Matthew 3:11, NASB). During our three-year tenure, many people were baptized in the Holy Spirit. These events occurred in the church, people's homes and wherever we were that people wanted that experience. The most common and obvious resulting evidence of the truth and reality of a person receiving this spiritual baptism is the person would begin speaking in "tongues," a new and spiritual prayer language.

At the church one morning during my prayer time, I was "talking to God." He made a reference to "when you enter the ministry." This shocked me. I said, "God, I have been pastoring this church for more than a year. I thought that I was already in the ministry."

"You are in training for the ministry." It was much later that I remembered God speaking to me when attending Rhema Bible Training Center. "You will pastor a church as part of your training for evangelism."

Pastoring at this church gave me all kinds of experiences working with people in the ministry. There were many positive experiences and some negative experiences. I was learning from each of them. Naturally, I like to recall the positive experiences and rejoice in them. Some of the negative experiences,

I would like to forget. I have prayed for forgiveness for those mistakes—bad decisions. Again, I learned from each of them. This was the seventh and final phase of formal training that God planned for me. I did not realize that until about three years later. It seemed that I continued to be in training. Will I ever learn enough—however much "enough" is?

After a year or more, it became very noticeable that many "drifters" would stop by the church, usually needing money to travel and encouragement or support of some kind. Their stories were so similar that after a period of time, I could tell them their story before they started talking. "My wife, family, employer [whoever they could blame their troubles on] have caused me so much trouble that I had to leave. I decided to go west, where there was pretty country, people were free, opportunities were better, and I could do what I wanted to do." The coast seemed to be a buffer. It was as far west as they could go. However, if their problems were really severe, it seemed that they migrated north. I concluded after dealing with many "drifters" that the Columbia River, 15 miles north of us, was a natural buffer and the drifters accumulated in the northwest corner of Oregon where Seaside is located. I mentioned this to a pastor located across the river in southwest Washington. He assured me these drifters cross the river. "I get my share of drifters, too!"

One drifter had such severe problems that he had left his home in Florida, worked his way to California, and then north to northern Oregon. He showed some initiative by picking up odd jobs in the area and making traveling money. His plan was to leave in a day or two when he finished the temporary job he was working on. I had let him sleep in the basement of the church. One day, he disappeared. My top-quality Makita power saw that I had inadvertently left in the basement disappeared, too. He had told me that his goal when leaving Florida was to make his way to Alaska and go to work on a fishing boat. I figured that was as far away as he could get from his Florida family and employer problems.

Local church leadership had warned Linda and me to be cautious about drifters and their sad stories. "They each have serious needs. But they will drain you and cause you problems if you show compassion." With our Christian compassion, where do you draw the line and say yes or no? Another lesson to be learned.

Linda and I both noticed that God's anointing on me had changed. The evangelist's anointing had lifted, and a pastor's anointing had descended on me. I became far more patient and compassionate than ever before. Linda noticed a gentleness in me that became prominent. As I worked with individuals to develop their spiritual knowledge and skills, it excited me to see them step out in faith and minister to one another and their other friends. My desire to develop ministers in the congregation was occurring. Love and compassion for people soon became much stronger.

Three years later, when God spoke to me and said, "You have finished your job. It is time to leave," it was close to two months before the new pastor transition could take place. During those two months, it was very obvious to me that the pastor anointing was lifting and being replaced by the evangelist anointing. I soon started becoming impatient and short-tempered with people. I wanted out of there. I could hardly wait until the new pastor got to Seaside and I could leave. My enduring patience was gone!

In Bible school, we had been taught that there was a separate and different anointing for each ministry gift. To experience the change was a much stronger and more lasting lesson.

We had moved to Seaside in our small eight by twenty-eight feet "pipeline travel trailer." No one in the congregation seemed to be aware or care that we needed a larger permanent house. Instead of entering our travel trailer, visitors would often stand outside the front door and talk for a few minutes. Apparently, they were uncomfortable coming inside the small trailer. Right or wrong, I got the impression that some of the people had this attitude: "Jerry and Linda are not going to be here long. They can hook onto their travel trailer and go back to Oklahoma anytime they want to. Why should I support them?"

One Sunday morning, a couple visited our church. They lived in Portland and were staying in their vacation home in Manzanita, a beach town twenty-two miles south of Seaside. The house was three blocks from the beach. It was built "upside down." That is, the two bedrooms and bathroom were downstairs. The living room and kitchen were upstairs with picture windows that provided a picturesque view of the tall spruce trees and a deck that afforded a partial view of the ocean. The small fireplace gave the living room a cozy effect.

A few months after their church visit, this attorney who owned the vacation home called. "I have started a business in

Baton Rouge, Louisiana, where I was raised. We do not plan to live in Oregon or vacation there for several years, if at all. If you are still living in your travel trailer and would like to move into our vacation home in Manzanita, call me. I will not charge rent and will even pay the utility bills." It did not take us long to accept their offer. We moved and lived there for one and a half years. After leaving the Seaside church, we stayed in Manzanita and were active in a church there.

The house in Manzanita was a blessing to us. We felt like, "If the people of the church in Seaside saw no need to provide housing for their pastor, God saw the need and provided very well for us."

———

Seaside, Oregon, was the first community south of Washington state that had a big natural beach. Its location was directly west of the Portland, Oregon/Vancouver, Washington, metropolitan area. As a result, this community of 5,000 to 6,000 people would sometimes double in numbers of people on weekends and number as many as 20,000 people on major holiday weekends. People from those areas often called the Seaside Chamber of Commerce, requesting a local pastor to perform weddings. I had put my name on the list to be called for any type of pastoral services by both local and out-of-town visitors. As a result, I was called to perform many weddings and occasional funerals. These pastoral events added to my "training" as a minister and my original calling as an evangelist. I never charged a set fee for these duties, but I always told the people that I would accept an offering of whatever amount they chose.

One Fourth of July holiday weekend, I had scheduled an 11:00 a.m. wedding in Portland. This was a one-hundred-and-fifty-mile round-trip. The couple had rented a hotel ballroom, catered lunch, and wet bar and either purchased or rented a very nice suit and wedding dress for the occasion. Our pastoral responsibilities included two one-hour marriage counseling sessions at the church in Seaside. When Linda and I were to leave, the groom explained that he really wanted to pay me well, but due to all the expenses incurred, he did not have much money left. He gave me $50.

We drove west to a home in the mountains near Seaside. A couple wanted to be married this same Fourth of July afternoon. Here lived two couples in the same house. Linda and I privately referred to them as our "Oregon Hillbillies." They had attended church a few times, and one of the couples asked us to perform a wedding for them. We agreed and held the required two one-hour marriage counseling sessions with them. Due to their "circumstances," it was necessary for us to drive the 50-mile round trip for each session in their mountain home. When we were ready to leave, the groom explained to me that he really wanted to pay me well. He wanted to pay me $75, half next Friday on his payday and the other half two weeks later, his next payday. I accepted his terms. We are still waiting for "Friday payday" to get here!

Linda and I decided to let these two Fourth of July events be part of our experiential training. We still find these to be amusing circumstances and experiences.

We had a man start attending our church. He had previously suffered a brain aneurysm and could no longer talk. This man was in his fifties and single. He was very pleasant and congenial and attended church regularly. I was very concerned with the man and began to give him private counsel. I explained to him that through faith in the love and power of God, he could regain his speech. It took some time to get the man in agreement with a miracle of God for him. Eventually, this man began to utter a few intelligible words. As time progressed, he began to express sentences. Later, he attended an overnight men's meeting with several of the local church members. At the men's meeting, he stood before the group of about one hundred men and gave a three-minute testimony, speaking clearly and intelligibly. God is still doing miracles today! Even after that miraculous recovery, something made him question my ministry, and he quit attending church. What a disappointment for me!

Reviewing those circumstances, I had this encouraging message come to me, "You shall go speak. You shall speak to one or two…"

Visiting with an acquaintance one day, he asked, "Are you having any unusual problems in the church?"

My reply was, "In a church, you have people. People always have problems of various kinds. Why do you ask?"

"There are two witches' covens that meet in the sand dunes about eight miles north of here every Saturday night. Every time they meet, they pray against you and your church."

I asked, "How do you know that?"

He stated, "I used to be one of them, and one of my friends still in the covens told me."

I said, "I must be doing something right and good for God if two witches' covens are regularly praying against me."

Previously, a Christian lady visiting the church from Portland had told me that there were demons in the church building. It had never occurred to me that demons would be in a church building. She offered to help me clean them out. We went from room to room, praying and commanding the demons to leave. This completed, there was an obviously refreshing atmosphere in the building. She told me, "You never know when demons may follow a visitor or congregation member into your church building." Periodically after that, Linda and I would go throughout the building doing a spiritual house cleaning.

The former youth minister, whom I had met in Mesa, Arizona, several years ago, called me. He was contracting house construction in his home area of Bozeman, Montana. He had ventured into construction of a steel-framed airplane hangar at the local airport. This being his first steel-framed building, he ran into some construction assembly problems that were different from wood-framed buildings. He called me requesting help. I had been a steel building construction contractor before entering the ministry. Drawing upon my previous experience and expertise, I assured the friend I could solve the assembly problems. I spent a week there and completed the building construction.

Driving home was a sixteen-hour trip. I left early Saturday morning, knowing that I was scheduled to preach Sunday morning. As I drove, I prayed for several hours "in my spirit language." This was January 9, 1996. As I prayed, I asked about the conditions of the church. God spoke to me clearly and distinctly in my spirit. He said, "You have done your job. Now it is time to go, time to leave this church." He did not say where we were to go or what we were to do. I asked who was to replace me. God replied, "Dale Proctor."

Dale and Karen Proctor were ministers from Grove, Oklahoma. They visited our church while on vacation in August 1995. We had met them only the one time. They had done missionary work in several countries. Their credentials and recommendations were commendable. I announced to the church the next morning that we were leaving and God had told me who the new pastor was to be. That afternoon, I called Dale and asked if he was interested in pastoring the Seaside church. Dale replied with a strong "Yes." Dale and Karen were very enthused when I told them that God had told me that they were to be the new pastors at River of Life Church. The transition Sunday was scheduled for February 4, 1996.

It is an understatement to say that pastoring a church was a unique experience. Whatever success we had during ten years of evangelism and three years of pastoring must be determined by the criteria of hearing from God and doing what He has told us to do. Often, man's criteria do not apply to ministry success or failure. Reviewing the three-year experience, I am well aware that if I faced some of the same situations again, I would likely make some different decisions and take different actions. The people who were critical of some of my decisions and actions were not aware of many of the details which often were private, and I would not reveal them. For the sake of the people involved, I kept those details private and tolerated the criticism that came. But yes, I made some mistakes.

Evangelism seems to flow freely out of me. Sharing the teaching and lifestyle of Jesus, the Christ, sharing one-on-one or in home Bible studies, and preaching in formal church situations are equally satisfying. Linda and I will continue to fulfill our basic call from God until we hear from Him concerning specific directions.

Epilogue

After leaving the church at Seaside, we did not have specific direction from God as to what to do or what direction to take in both ministry and life in general. We stayed in Manzanita, serving that pastor and church. We also did evangelism ministry locally, in central Oregon, and wherever that took us. To make a living, I had a job driving an 18-wheel truck hauling fresh-caught fish from the fish-loading docks to the fish processing plants. Dependent on the type of fish caught, we delivered to processing plants located as far north as the Canadian border and as far south as the California border. Driving the coastal mountain highways both in summer and with winter's snow and ice on the mountain highways while attempting to stay on schedule with loads of ice-covered fish was another unique experience in this preacher's life. The apostle Paul plied his trade as a tent maker while ministering. I drove trucks.

We chose to move back to northeast Oklahoma, our original home area. Kids and grandkids wanted our time and attention. After six years in Oregon, we also needed their attention and wanted fellowship with our family.

At various times we have needed to use each of the lessons learned during these "Seven Phases of Training" and sometimes felt as though we needed much more knowledge. During those times, we cried out to God, seeking His wisdom, authority, power, action, and love. God is always faithful to our calls. He "makes things happen" in our times of need. Wherever we go, God is there with us using His supernatural power.

Since leaving Seaside, Oregon, and completing the Seven Phases of Training designated by God, Linda and I have traveled to a total of sixteen countries on thirty-five mission trips. People in those sixteen countries have been ministered to however we understood God directing us. God is still working through His ministers today with His supernatural miracles. By the power of the Holy Spirit and in the name of Jesus, we have experienced blind eyes open in minutes, cataracts removed within five days, deaf ears opened, arthritis removed within minutes and many kinds of illnesses healed. Certainly, anything in a supernatural or miraculous manner that happens when we have ministered, *we give God all the glory!* Linda and I do not know how to perform the supernatural or miraculous. But we do choose to be faithful and obedient to Him and His call on our lives. Another book will detail some of the miracles God performed on these past trips.

What about the two prophecies stating, "You will lead a nation to Christ," and God waking me three mornings in a row in Honolulu, Hawaii, showing me the same message in the Bible? That happening and the timing of that happening is dependent on God. His original message to "Go speak…" is still prominent to me.

So, what happens next? Undoubtedly, God will direct us. Linda and I will be patient, obedient, and faithful to go wherever and whenever He tells us and do whatever He tells us. As we have heard Rev. Kenneth E. Hagin say, "God did not tell me to retire. He told me to *refire!*"

About the Author

Jerry Clark and his wife, Linda, reside in the northeast Oklahoma town of Chelsea. Jerry was a teacher, football coach, and principal for twelve years. He also was a steel building contractor for seven years. His wife, Linda, taught math in the public schools eighteen years.

On September 25, 1982, God spoke to Jerry "in a clear, distinct and audible voice" and told him to "Go speak—." Jerry closed his steel building business and moved his family to Broken Arrow, Oklahoma, where he and Linda were graduated from Rhema Bible Training College.

They are evangelists, having ministered in sixteen American states and sixteen countries during thirty-five mission trips. Currently they do local evangelism, have invitations to three African countries, do zoom meetings, and are writing books concerning the ministry.

Printed in the USA
CPSIA information can be obtained
at www.ICGtesting.com
LVHW022047040624
782274LV00011B/193